STEP

RIGHT IN

1.   **ALLAN KAPROW.** Coca-Cola, Shirley Cannonball? 1960. Happening

2. JEAN FOLLETT. Lady with Open-Door Stomach. 1955. 47 x 48". Assemblage

5

3. ROBERT RAUSCHENBERG.
Interview. 1955. 66 x 49 x 12". Combine (Assemblage)

4. GLORIA GRAVES.

Little Clara's Room. 1960.

5 x 7 x 8". Assemblage

5.   ALLAN KAPROW. Grandma's Boy. 1957. 18½ x 15½ x 12½". Assemblage

ENTRANCES AND ENCLOSURES

6.   RED GROOMS. The Burning Building. 1959. Happening

7. ROBERT WHITMAN.
Mouth. 1961. Happening

LITTLE
MAN

IN
BIG
SEA

8. JACKSON POLLOCK.

The Artist at Work. 1950.

Environmental Painting

9.   RENEE MILLER. Bug, Mask, and Stars. 1960.

53½ x 54 x 2″. Extension Painting

12

**BECOMING
THE**

10. **MARTHA EDELHEIT. Frabjous Day. 1960. c. 60 x 42″. Construction**

11. ALLAN KAPROW.

Garage Environment. 1960.

Environment

ENVIRONMENT

14

12, 13.   **ALLAN KAPROW.** **An Apple Shrine. 1960. Environment**

AND THE HAPPENING

15. JIM DINE. The House. 1960. Environment

NOTE ON THE PHOTOGRAPHS

Photographs of art works have their own reality and sometimes they are art in turn. Those taken of the subject of this book tend to be particularly free. They refer to their models, but strangely, as would a movie taken of a dream, stopped at unexpected intervals. A movie of a dream cannot be the dream, and a frame, here and there pulled from it, must leave the viewer guessing even more. Yet guessing is dreaming too, and if we can never know another man's dream as he knows it, we can come close to the spirit of his activity by engaging in a similar process. Beyond art, sharing in dream processes is probably what we call reality.

I have put together these photographs, therefore, in a way that would encourage such reverie. The result, in my view, comes close to the character and meaning of the individual works, as well as their larger relations to each other and to a moment in time. Conventional grouping of data in chronological order has been perfectly valid; but this is dreaming also, and I have watched this reel too many times to pay attention any longer.

16. CLARENCE SCHMIDT.

Untitled. 1930 (?). Environment

SPECTERS

FROM REFUSE

17. JIM DINE. Bedspring. 1960. Assemblage

18. **RED GROOMS.** The Burning Building. 1959. Happening

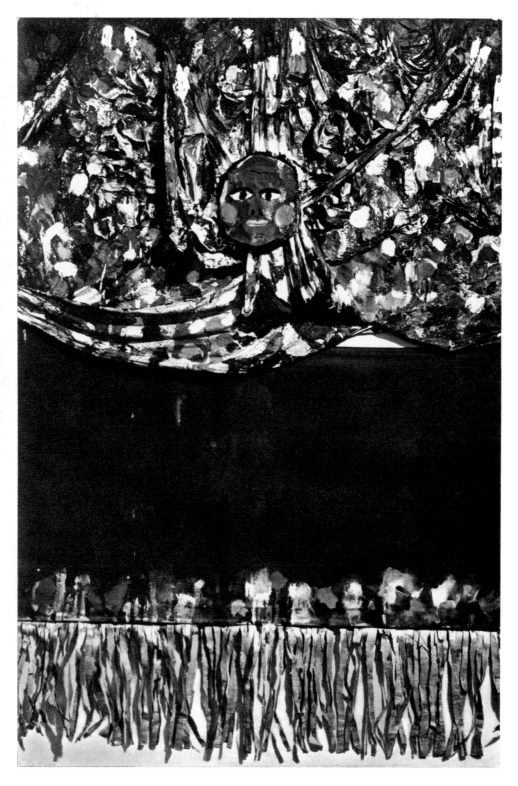

19.   JIM DINE. The Gypsy. 1959. 4′ x 5′ x 3″. Assemblage

OBSESSION

20, 21. YAYOI KUSAMA.

From The Driving Image show.

1964. Environment

28

ENCHANTMENT

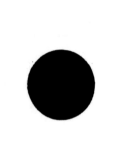

23. JIM DINE. The House. Environment (in progress)

24. JIM DINE. The House. 1960.

Bringing materials for Environment

(outside Judson Gallery)

OUT OF GUTTERS AND GARBAGE CANS

25.   **CLAES OLDENBURG.** The Street. 1960. Bringing materials for Environment (outside Judson Gallery)

34

26. CLAES OLDENBURG.

Snapshots from the City. 1960.

Happening (from The Street)

27.   **GEORGE SEGAL. Dinner Table. 1961. Environmental Sculpture**

STATUES INSIDE

28.   ALLAN KAPROW. Eat. 1964. Environment

29. **ALLAN KAPROW.** Eat. 1964. Environment

30. **ROBERT WHITMAN.** Untitled. 1958. 6′ x 6′ x 6′. Assemblage

FRAGILE

GEOMETRIES

42

31, 32.   AY-O. Hydra (and others). 1962. 7' x 7'. Environmental Sculpture

FICTIONS

AND IMMATERIAL

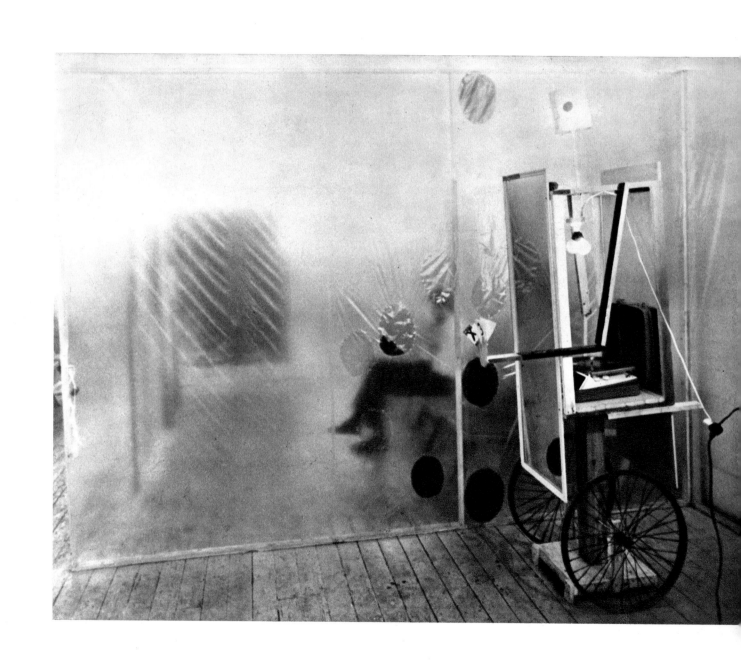

SPACES

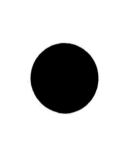

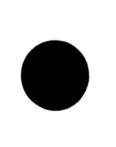

35. JEAN FOLLETT. Title unknown. 1955(?). c. 5′ x 7′. Assemblage

48

OBJECTS HUNG ON PANEL

**DAYS TO
BE MOVED**

36. GEORGE BRECHT.

Blair. 1959. c. 5' x 1½' x 2".

Rearrangeable Assemblage

PANELS TO REARRANGE

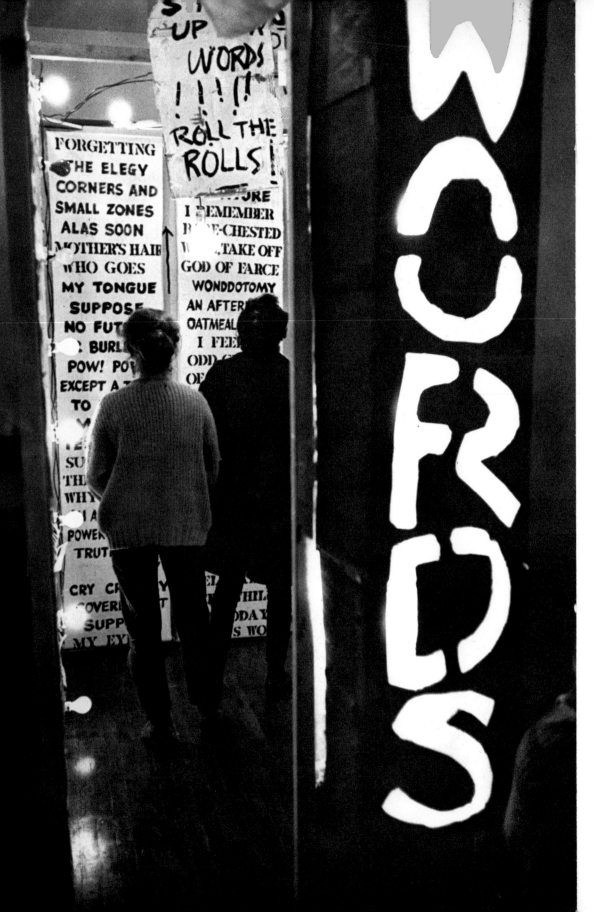

38.   ALLAN KAPROW. Words. 1961.

Rearrangeable Environment

with lights and sounds

39.   ALLAN KAPROW. Penny Arcade (detail). 1956. Assemblage with lights and sounds

WORDS

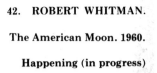

42. ROBERT WHITMAN.

The American Moon. 1960.

Happening (in progress)

CAVES

PREVIOUS PAGE:

43. **ROBERT WHITMAN.** The American Moon. 1960. Happening

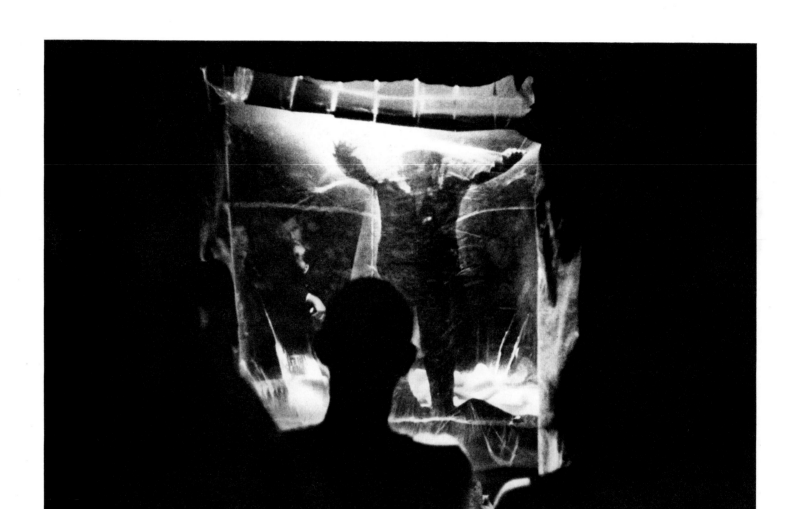

44. **ROBERT WHITMAN.** The American Moon. 1960. Happening

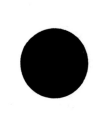

CHRYSALIS

45, 46. ROBERT WHITMAN.

The American Moon. 1960. Happening

47. ROBERT WHITMAN. Mouth. 1961. Happening

ANIMALS

THE ANIMAL NODS, SINGS, JIGS

8. **ROBERT WATTS.** Victory. 1960. c. 7′ x 6′ x 1′.

Assemblage with sounds, movement, lights

ENDLESS

**JAZZ MAN
BLOWS**

**CARS
TOPPLE
HAY**

TREE ARMY READY

TREE MAN TOPPLES POLES

50–53. ALLAN KAPROW.

Tree. 1963. Happening

AFTERMATH

54. ALLAN KAPROW. Tree. 1963. Happening

55.   ALLAN KAPROW. Chicken. 1962. Happening (in rehearsal)

HANGING THINGS

56.   ROBERT WHITMAN. The American Moon. 1960. Happening

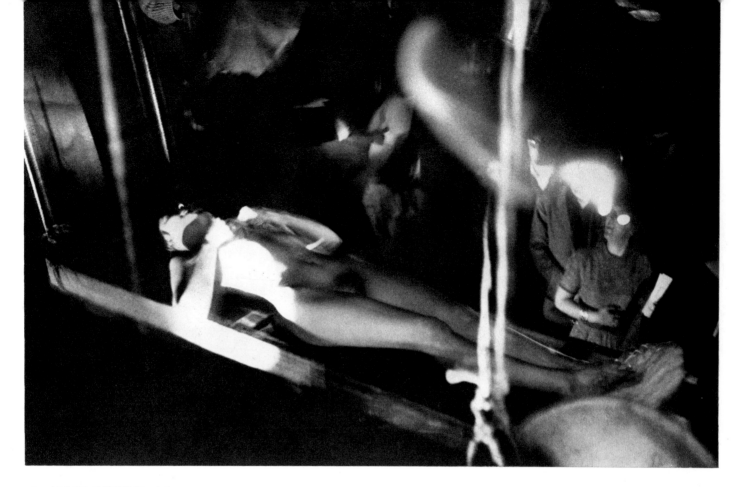

57.   ALLAN KAPROW. A Service for the Dead (1). 1962. Happening

58, 59.   ALLAN KAPROW.   A Service for the Dead (1). 1962. Happening

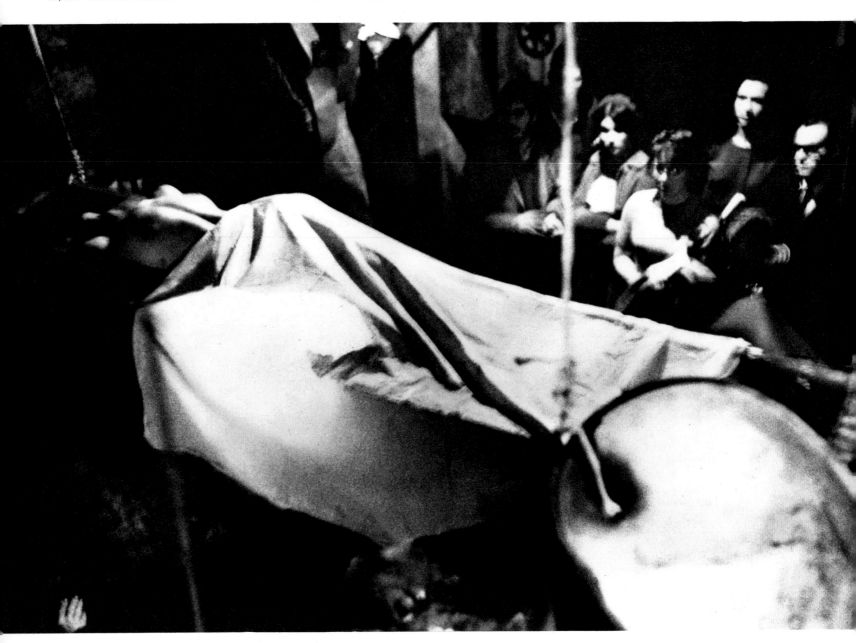

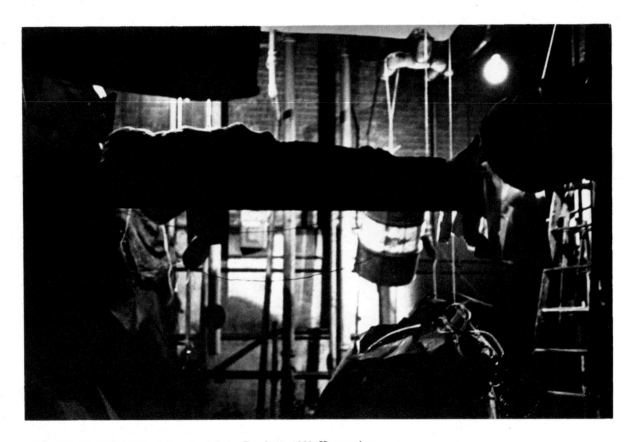

60.   ALLAN KAPROW. A Service for the Dead (1). 1962. Happening

A FACE IN THE WALL

61. RED GROOMS. The Burning Building. 1959. Happening

62. JEAN FOLLETT. Many-Legged Creature. 1955. 40 x 48″. Mixed media

SPIDER

WEB

63. CLARENCE SCHMIDT.

Untitled. 1930(?). Environment

64, 65.   CLARENCE SCHMIDT.

Untitled. 1930(?). Environment

86

MIRROR

THE WORLD

66.   GEORGE SEGAL. Filling Station. 1963. Environmental Sculpture

DRINK PAINT

ENJOY WORK

67.   JIM DINE. The Smiling Workman.

1960. Happening

RIGHT:

68.   JIM DINE. The House. 1960.

Environment (in progress)

69. **ALLAN KAPROW.** Orange. 1964. Happening

BATHTUB

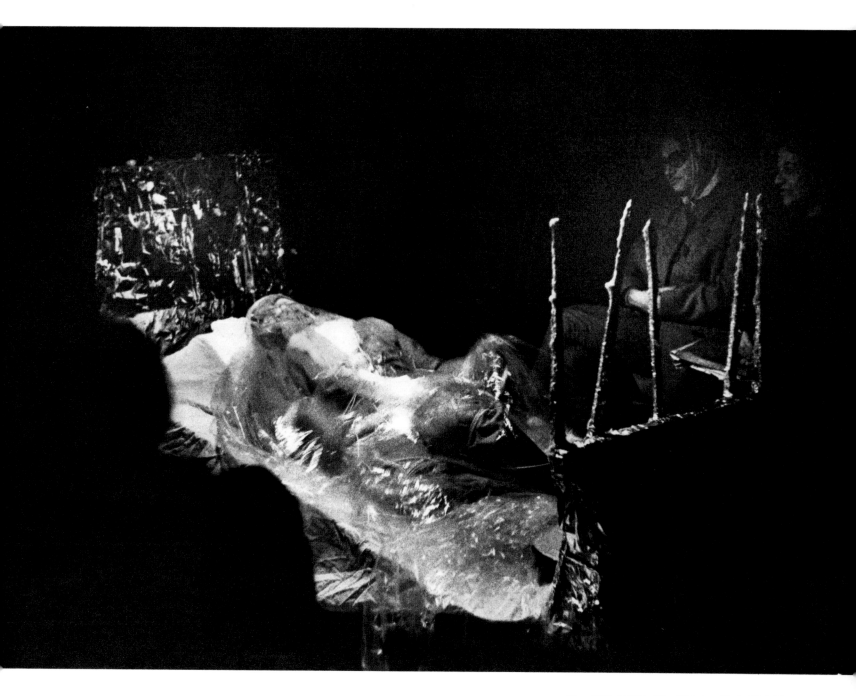

70.   JIM DINE. The Shining Bed. 1960. Happening

BED

71. ALLAN KAPROW. Bon Marché. 1963. Happening

BAPTISM

72.   ALLAN KAPROW. A Service for the Dead (2). 1962. Happening

73–75.   ALLAN KAPROW. A Service for the Dead (2). 1962. Happening

BURIAL

76.   ALLAN KAPROW.   A Service for the Dead (2). 1962. Happening

AND IMMOLATION

CHICKEN
MAN CROWS

77, 78.   ALLAN KAPROW.

Chicken. 1962. Happening

RIOTERS
OVERTURN
CAGE

COP
SPRAYS
GAS

79. ALLAN KAPROW.

Chicken. 1962. Happening

80.   JEAN FOLLETT. Gulliver. 1956. c. 4′ x 8′. Assemblage

MECHANICAL DREAMS

81.   JEAN TINGUELY. Hommage à New York: A Self-Constructing, Self-Destroying Work of Art. 1960. Assemblage in motion

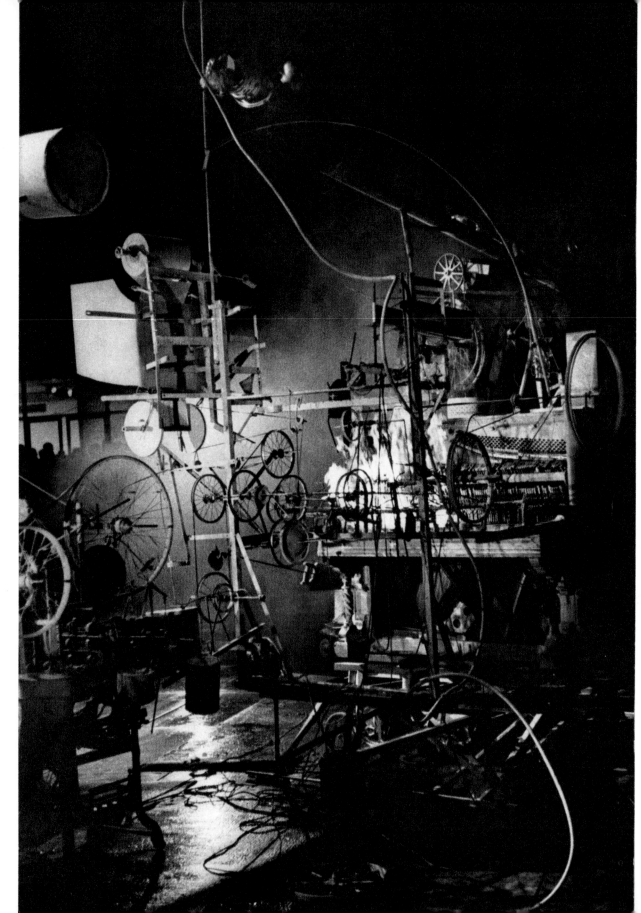

82. JEAN TINGUELY.

Hommage à New York:

A Self-Constructing,

Self-Destroying Work of Art.

1960. Assemblage in motion

83. CLARENCE SCHMIDT. Untitled. 1930(?). Environment

84, 85.   CLARENCE SCHMIDT. Untitled. 1930(?). Environme

BECOME
PATCHWORK
MEMORIES

86, 87.   GEORGE SEGAL and RUTH SCHMIDT (collaborators). Ruth, in Her Kitchen. 1964. Sculpture and Environment

88. **ROBERT RAUSCHENBERG.** Untitled. 1954–55.

c. 6′ x 3′ x 2′. Combine (Assemblage)

89, 90. CLARENCE SCHMIDT.

Untitled. 1930(?). Environment

TANGLES

AND PATHS

91, 92. ALLAN KAPROW.

An Apple Shrine. 1960. Environment

118

TO

THE SHRINE

93. ALLAN KAPROW. A Spring Happening. 1961. Happening (in rehearsal)

LAWNMOWER SCREAMS

94. ALLAN KAPROW. Eat. 1964. Environment

IN THE STOCKADE

95. ALLAN KAPROW. A Spring Happening. 1961. Happening (in rehearsal)

AND WALLS FALL DOWN

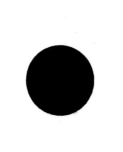

96.   ALLAN KAPROW. Bon Marché. 1963. Happening

DEBRIS

AND DEBRIS

97. CLAES OLDENBURG. Ironworks. 1961. Happening

98. GEORGE SEGAL. Bus Driver. 1962. Environmental Sculpture

AND MADMEN

99. CLAES OLDENBURG. Foto-Death. 1961. Happening

EMBLEMS

100, 101. JIM DINE.

Car Crash. 1960. Happening

SHUDDER

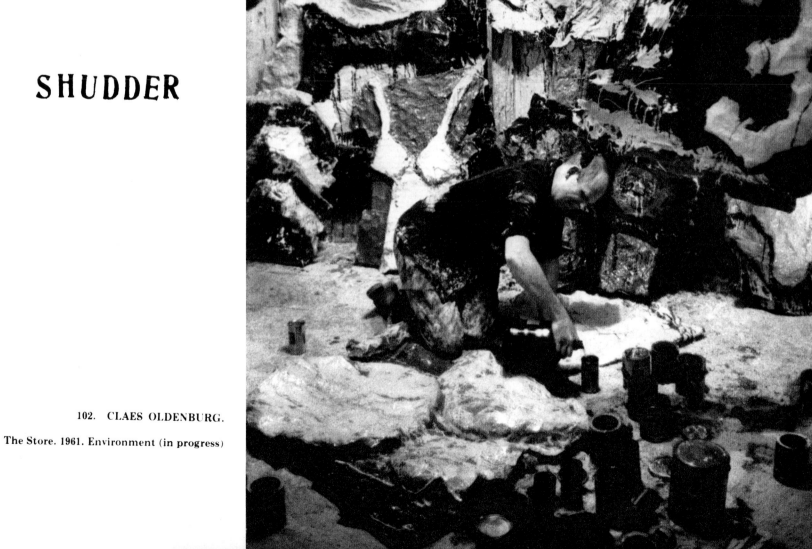

102. CLAES OLDENBURG.

The Store. 1961. Environment (in progress)

THE TIRE
SWINGS

103, 104.   ALLAN KAPROW.

Courtyard. 1962. Happening

OVER THE
MOUNTAIN

136

105. ALLAN KAPROW.

Courtyard. 1962. Happening

106. ROBERT RAUSCHENBERG. Monogram. 1959. c. 7′ x 7′ x 3′. Combine (Assemblage)

107.   JIM DINE. Car Crash. 1960. Happening (in rehearsal)

108. ALLAN KAPROW.

Yard. 1961. Environment

RECALLING THE ACT

109. ALLAN KAPROW. Yard. 1961. Environment

OF ART

110. CLAES OLDENBURG.

The Store. 1961. Environment (in progress)

111. JACKSON POLLOCK

The Artist at Work. 1950.

Environmental Painting

112. ALLAN KAPROW.

Yard. 1961.

Environment

113. ALLAN KAPROW. Yard. 1961. Environment

SO STEP RIGHT IN

ASSEMBLAGE,

WITH A SELECTION
OF SCENARIOS BY:

9 JAPANESE OF THE
GUTAI GROUP

JEAN-JACQUES LEBEL

WOLF VOSTELL

GEORGE BRECHT

KENNETH DEWEY

MILAN KNÍŽÁK

ALLAN KAPROW

HARRY N. ABRAMS, INC., PUBLISHERS

ENVIRONMENTS

& HAPPENINGS

TEXT AND DESIGN
BY ALLAN KAPROW

NEW YORK

LIBRARY OF CONGRESS CATALOG CARD NUMBER: 65-17018

All rights reserved. No part of the contents of this book may
be reproduced without the written permission of the publishers
HARRY N. ABRAMS, INC., NEW YORK
Printed and bound in Japan

CONTENTS

PREFACE

THIS BOOK *is an introduction to a recent development in the arts. It concentrates on the background, the theory, and some of the implications of these developments. Beyond a brief example here and there, it does not attempt to study particular works, sketching out, instead, an overall view. In the near future, analyses of individual artists will be possible, but not before the nature of the work done is defined and made familiar.*

The book, furthermore, is not intended to be a summary after the fact. It has been written in the midst of a young activity, with an interest that was both observant and highly biased. Being part of the activity, I was inclined to look at and judge an art-in-the-making as well as influence its course. Artists, like critics and historians, make the history they reflect, even with the best of intentions to remain objective. I thought, when I began writing, that I should try both to observe and to influence as much as possible.

But any book conceived in the middle of things rapidly evolving is bound to be topical and incomplete. This is its obvious limitation, as well as its special merit, since no later history can quite capture its special urgency or its contemporary flavor. This book was largely written in 1959 at the suggestion of Max and Anita Baker, who were the directors of the Reuben Gallery in New York City, where much of the art discussed here was centered, and it was finished in the next year. It was then revised in 1961 in accordance with what was happening in art and with the changes in my own mind. Now, much that was only a glimmer in the late fifties has become clearer. My convictions have become sharper, and my demands upon my own work, and that of others, more severe. And so I revised the book once again. Now that it is to be published, it will have to remain a document of these last few years. If I wrote it again it would be a different book.

ART AND ARCHITECTURE

A critical turning point has been reached in a major area of avant-garde effort, which I believe is entirely to the good but which is forcing upon us the possibly disagreeable task of revising some cherished assumptions regarding the nature of the plastic arts.

Certain advanced works being done at this moment are rapidly losing their traditional identities and something else, quite far-reaching in its implications, is taking their place.

On the one hand, looking broadly at the whole of recent modern art, the differences which were once so clear between graphic art and painting have practically been eliminated; similarly, the distinctions between painting and collage, between collage and construction, between construction and sculpture, and between some large constructions and a quasi architecture. Even the late work of Le Corbusier has been called habitable sculpture. In keeping with all of this is a remarkable and pervasive taste for unmeasurable and irregular forms as well as formats.

On the other hand—though much is still on paper or in conversation—architecture as such is about to come to grips with what Frank Lloyd Wright only incompletely dreamed of, an organism which would flow from part to part, not only easily within itself, but within the forms of nature (now quite possible with sprayed plastic and concrete techniques). The mood is growing among some younger architects to leave the contemporary "neoclassic" style, and to question the sacrosanct rectangle and arc which, with their variations, have dominated the shape of the art almost since its origins. Instead of a compass-and-ruler style, they are seeking one whose forms would emerge more from the feel of nature itself in all its variety and sense of the spontaneous and unplanned. When this happens, nature and architecture may truly (and not tentatively as in Bear Run and Taliesin West) become continuous with one another. The movement in this direction has already begun in the other media.

This continuity is significant, the critical issue in fact; for drawing and painting, and in a large measure sculpture and the so-called minor arts, have until now been completely dependent upon the conditions set down by the structure of the house: one need only imagine a canvas without a flat wall and the cubic enframement of the room, a chair on an irregular floor. . . . Artists for at least a century have worked as though the only thing of importance were the work in front of them, a world unto itself. Yet it is no accident that painters and critics have been deeply disturbed by the curved walls and spiral ramp of the Guggenheim Museum for precisely these infractions of "unquestionable" prerequisites. The strong tie to a traditional architectural matrix lies very close to the surface of independence.

Hence, when architecture becomes organic to the degree that the other plastic arts have, then probably the blurring of boundaries in those will extend to include it. In such new circumstances a traditional painting would contrast with the space that flowed about it. I do not of course insist that this is necessarily bad. We are accustomed to the potpourri idea as well; and we also shall be surrounded by conventional architecture for a long time, enough time to amply justify the continuation of "paintings," "sculpture," "prints," etc. But I am saying that it is important to recognize very clearly how deeply involved with each other on a primary level the plastic arts have been. Once you change the conditions for one, you imply a conflict (a contrast at least, which is enough to call attention to the change) in the other. And these conditions are without any doubt changing now.

There is a twist in the order of events here, however. If I have said that at root paintings, etc., could not possibly exist in their form up to the present without the psychological and physical definition of space given to them by architecture; and if Wright arrogantly referred to architecture as the "mother art," he was correct only with respect to sources, for historical development has shifted the shoe to the other foot. We must not forget that children leave the home and sometimes much later return to mother the aged parent. It is well known that because of serious practical problems which prevent quick response to new experience, architecture must develop comparatively slowly. One of the most advanced buildings actually built to date is probably Le Corbusier's church at Ronchamp, and its forms and their relationships are those of the period 1917 to 1925. A glance at the paintings of that era will confirm this.

It appears, therefore, that what I call the "private" plastic arts are able to chart a day-by-day course, producing innovations that are possible because it costs little to do so and only one person is initially involved. In their present radical form they are probably predicting the future look of architecture, and they are doing so by ignoring the house in which they have for so long been nurtured.

For as each new exhibition of this recent work has proven, it is becoming harder and harder to arrange a show without compromising present needs with older methods. The work never looks quite right; it fits uncomfortably within the glaring geometry of the gallery box, and some artists have already tried camouflage of various kinds in an attempt to obliterate this discrepancy. The

153

studio was always better, however basically similar the architectural elements, because there the clutter of old and new work, arranged unconsciously perhaps, had gradually erased much of that uncomfortable sense of ruled enframement. In short, contemporary art has moved out of its traditional limits. Painting, which has been without question the most advanced and experimental of the plastic arts, has over and over provoked the question, "Should the format or field always be the closed, flat rectangle?" by utilizing gestures, scribblings, large scales with no frame, which suggest to the observer that both the physical and metaphysical substance of the work continue indefinitely in all directions beyond the canvas. (See my article, "The Legacy of Jackson Pollock," *Art News*, October, 1958.)

More recently, a large body of diverse compositions referred to as Combines (Robert Rauschenberg's name for his own work), Neo-Dada, or Assemblage employs a variety of materials and objects in an equally varied range of formats, completely departing from the accepted norms required by "painting" as we have known it. But this has brought sharply into focus the fact that *the room has always been a frame or format too,* and that this shape is inconsistent with the forms and expression emerging from the work in question.

Of course, some artists find a positive value in this contradiction and make use of it, as another generation (Pollock's, for example) used the confines of the canvas as the only limit to an intrinsically limitless form; much the same is true in jazz, whose beat is the constant which defines the degree of freedom achieved in improvisation. These relatively unchanging factors are felt to be a kind of home base. Yet this may be temporary, a transitional value for today, since a number of younger artists do not find such methods acceptable any longer; they feel them to be excess baggage at least, which often involves needless discords with the past, in which these methods originated. If there are to be measures and limits in art they must be of a new kind. Rather than fight against the confines of a typical room, many are actively considering working out in the open. They cannot wait for the new architecture.

It should be evident from the foregoing that this suggests a crisis of sorts. Quite apart from the aesthetic re-evaluation it forces upon us, its immediate practical effect is to render the customary gallery situation obsolete.

What is important is to examine in some specific detail the principles involved, particularly with respect to painting. For the painters, with the relatively greater freedom their medium has allowed, have led the movement that has tended to erase the borders between their art and its related media.

THE FIELD IN PAINTING

From time immemorial picture making, in all its vicissitudes, has maintained a hands-off policy respecting two elements: the symmetrical geometric (usually rectangular, oval, or square) field, and the flat surface. The reasons for this are subtle but not difficult. Since around 1400 B.C., when Egypt and Crete were already using what we can term a conventional picture area, that is, when the image was enclosed within a predesignated boundary, the nature of the field as a unique metaphor of the real and total world has been clear, even if it remained below the threshold of most analysis.

Much earlier a bison was painted on a cave wall, and in the flickering torch light, molded to the bumps of the natural rock, overlapping other previously painted animals, lost here and there in shadow, the image was almost indistinguishable from its surroundings. Either it was experienced as real substance in real space (having magical powers) or the image was the entire "picture" (assuming that at certain times it was seen *as a picture* of a bison). In the latter instance it existed in no space except the space within the animal's own outline.

When next a horizon line was drawn under a cow, the separation of image from environment occurred like a logical thunderbolt, and thereafter painting (and man) could never be the same. Painting had become symbol rather than power, i.e., something which *stood for* experience rather than *acting directly upon* it.

It was only a series of steps before the horizon was joined to three other lines at right angles to each other (at first representing a corral, the emergence of the concept of property?) and the rectangular field was there to stay. Objects on or within this shape constituted the whole story of humankind and its relation to the universe. It was a useful convention, since the form of that field hardly resembled the more organic stuff of nature. And thus a sort of psychological truce-for-a-moment with reality was enacted every time one looked at a painting.* One agreed in effect to the purely mental invention of the painting field as the only possible way to *refer* to the unseeable boundary of the known world. For indeed, painters realized early that you could not literally imitate nature.

The flatness of the surface—also unlike accepted experience—guaranteed that this intellectual realm would not be contradicted by the images placed within its boundaries. Here the picture emerged complete, a painted imagery in an unnatural space at once flat and by suggestion also three-dimensional. The drama of

* "Painting" is not necessarily "picture making," for the first man to decorate his body and personal implements was *ipso facto* a "painter." Painting *came to mean* making pictures, and this special form is now beginning to dissolve. The history of painting may be viewed as a pictorial balance established between man and the world which surrounds him. In terms of the familiar object–ground problem, all objects may be interpreted to symbolize the human being and his experience, while all grounds of "negative space" around objects may stand for his conception of the universe. In some periods, such as the ancient Greek, the image dominates the field and man sees himself controlling the world. In others, like the medieval, the field dominates the image, hence the world constricts the human. And in yet others, such as the late pagan and early Christian, there is a potent ambiguity. This seems to hold true today as well.

painting has always been the juggling of these paradoxes of the seemingly real and the symbol for the real.

The Middle Ages were typically less strict in their application of the "rules" regarding the integrity of the surface and medium of painting. Angels' and madonnas' heads were often surrounded by raised, gilded-stucco halos. However, it was usually limited to this special subject matter, as though to render that most intangible of phenomena—a radiance—more factual. But the more classical tradition, by which we have been dominated, assumed in one way or another a set of harmonies or unities, viz., time and place, form and subject matter, surface and field, field and the room it was placed in. By 1912 or 1913, the medium of collage really began to break the rules, though, by our standards, modestly. Most of the area of those collages was conventionally pictorial, and the paper additions were neatly pasted down so as to disturb the surface only a little. The damage, however, was done. Which was the real—the paper that, as a substance, was different from the canvas; the cut-out image which began on the paper and merged with the painted image on the canvas; or the print on the paper which told you it was wallpaper or an advertisement (from the outside, *realer* world) and thus could not be part of painting? All was kept precariously in check by the conventional shape of the field. To alter this by making it organic or irregular would be, as many current experimenters have found out, to discover that the painting became a single painted thing rather than a reference to objects in space. And this would provoke quite different responses than those conventionally required for painting.

It took the Cubist constructions, and thereafter their Dada and Surrealist modifications, to predict a clear break with painting without simply going to sculpture, although painting surely still dominated the scene.

Since World War II, with the collages and constructions created in the United States, a big step was taken. Unencumbered by ancient local traditions, and fortified by a recent graft of Surrealist adventurousness, these works immediately became freer in scope, looser in form, and larger in scale than anything Europe had produced. Most telling was the fact that this not-quite-painting became an exclusive rather than a marginal mode of working for many American artists.

Once this took place, the very qualities which make painting a distinct medium vanished, and artists were faced with various problems. If the edges of pasted matter on a collage were left sticking up far enough, that exquisite balance achieved by Cubism's use of pictorial space and real space would be destroyed— low relief sculpture of a sort would result. The field no longer functioned in the spatial way it could in an older painting. The same thing happened if you cut holes in the canvas and the wall showed through. It felt wrong, and only by moving the canvas a few feet out from the wall could you accept what you saw behind it as equivalent in value to what took place on its surface (for now other objects, colors, moving people, etc., could be seen through the holes, rather than the dead end of the blank wall surface). But at this point the canvas's affinity with the wall was broken and a new disturbance was felt in the attention called to the canvas itself as object. Such a "painting" was ambiguous in its role, suggesting vaguely a banner, medallion, or room partition. If the shape of the field was altered irregularly, supposing that this change would compensate for the disturbance, its object-nature rather than field-nature became only the more apparent. The further introduction of other foreign matter (wood, straw, bulbs, shoes, machine parts, etc.) only enhanced the dilemma.

A dilemma for some, who gave up the whole problem as a lost cause and returned to more conventional methods, but an escape hatch for others, who were looking for a new way of working that would avoid the restrictions imposed by "pure" painting. Some interesting alternatives emerged, leading in different directions, but all of them involved *relinquishing the goal of picture making entirely* by accepting the possibilities that lay in using a broken surface and a nongeometric field.

THE NEW FORMS, MATERIALS, AND ATTITUDES

The alternatives turned out to be what are now called Assemblages and Environments. They are at root the same—the only difference is one of size. Assemblages may be handled or walked around, while Environments must be walked into. Though scale obviously makes all the experiential difference in the world, a similar form principle controls each of these approaches, and some artists work in both with great ease.

This principle may be named simply *extension*. Molecule-like, the materials (including paint) at one's disposal grow in any desired direction and take on any shape whatsoever. In the freest of these works the field, therefore, is created as one goes along, rather than being there *a priori*, as in the case of a canvas of certain dimensions. It is a process, and one that works from the inside out, though this should be considered merely metaphorical, rather than descriptive, since there actually exists no inside, a bounded area being necessary to establish a field. There are only a few elements one begins with, and these at best are located with respect to one's body and the room itself. Thus, if extension is the principle, it "begins" much less definitely than the first mark placed upon a canvas, whose relations to the outer edges are quickly weighed by any competent painter. However, unless one works out in the open, it must be admitted that old responses geared to a canvas's dimensions and character are probably now transferred to the three-dimensional measurements of the room, and this may be a response to a "field." But it is a different point of departure from the accepted pictorial one, being basically environmental. Perhaps the domains of sculpture, interior design, and architecture are suggested here, but as respects the latter two, the work at the moment is in every practical sense "useless" and uninhabitable, and in the instance of sculpture there are some striking differences which shall be noted shortly. In any event, a fuller involvement with actual space is important.

This space is in part the literal distance between all solids included in the work. But it is also a space that is a direct heritage of painting—therefore it is important to remember that the innovations which are under discussion have primarily grown out of the advanced painting of the last decade. For purely pictorial phenomena play a strong part. Effects of a painterly kind occur when two or more separated objects containing one or more elements in common (say the color red) appear to contradict or warp the literal space by the tendency of the mind to resolve them into a single spatial unit. This is quite similar to using a red in the foreground of a picture and the same color in the background, which allows them to be seen as one plane, thus restoring "flatness" to the painting even while it is three-dimensional. However, here the inclusion of palpable distances not only increases the levels of ambiguity already present in pictorial solutions, but these distances in turn are highly unstable because the viewer may constantly change his vantage point.

Within this context, color itself enjoys the full range that it has always had in

160

painting. It may define a surface (as a coat of paint on a chair), evoke a filmlike atmosphere or glaze, or saturate a whole substance with its properties. (It therefore can play in and out of space without regard for the actual positions of its occurrence). Needless to say, all the sensations of heat, fragrance, taste, weight, and motion, and all the more subtle symbolical overtones of color, with which we are already familiar, are not only amplified but warped in these new circumstances. We become aware of this when a balance is achieved between the application of color to one's materials and the prior existence of color in those materials (such as a black hat or silver foil). In other words, an object or area is often left unpainted because it either is already painted (a part of a car fender, for instance) or it has a color that permeates its entire body, as Jello, for example. This is considered to be as natural as making a painted area, and thus results in a give-and-take between the ready-made and the newly created. The expressiveness of color is consequently not only a product of hand and imagination; it is also a caprice of the accidental confluence of artfulness with a hundred other things "outside" art.

These things may include clothing, baby carriages, machine parts, masks, photographs, printed words, and so forth, which have a high degree of associational meaning; however, they may just as often be more generalized, like plastic film, cloth, raffia, mirrors, electric lights, cardboard, or wood—somewhat less specific in meaning, restricted to the substances themselves, their uses, and modes of transformation. There is no apparent theoretical limit to what may be used.

In practice, however, it must be stated that the very great majority of works which are composed of such stuff, both in New York City and throughout the world, have a fairly limited iconography: faded photos, old books, bottles, stuffed animals, old utensils, printed gingham, wallpaper and lacework, broken jewelry, toys-become-fetishes, boxes and drawers of mementos, dried flowers, bric-a-brac and keepsakes, etc., etc., all possessing a post-Surrealist nostalgia, a mood of reverie and gentle humor or irony. Some of these are authentically evocative and strange, yet most are weak when compared with their Dada and Surrealist prototypes. Their effect is one of charm rather than shock or transport; spiritually they are bloodless and cute and, naturally, are cultivated by the over-sophisticated and chic sets in international society. Yet the possibilities inherent in compositions of diverse materials are still abundant to a more exploratory mind. If an artist is alert to what is becoming worn out through too much usage, or to what has become downright cliché, he can always count on being in a position to examine the fresher alternatives that still lie untapped.

It can now be seen that what differentiates some of the smaller Assemblages from sculpture, as they are sometimes labeled, is just this range and use of materials. Modern sculpture still preserves the assumed sacrosanct unity and permanence of its medium: metal, stone, wood, plastic, or glass. And of course professional sculptors have pretty much eschewed color since the Middle Ages; those who have ventured into this territory have at best been tentative and at worst have used it only skin-deep. Finally, a conservative streak of the modern sculptor is seen in the all too frequent use of bases and stands, a holdover from monuments of the past with their elaborate pedestals. This by now vapid manner of distinguishing or glorifying a work is sculpture's homologue to the frame in painting, serving to separate it more definitely from reality. Contrasted to this, the best indoor Assemblages are either hung casually on the wall or from the ceiling, or are simply placed on the floor like any natural object or group of objects, for the floor is already a base too much. Out of doors, on the street or ground, few of these problems are posed.

Assemblages presently have several forms, some more radical than others. There are those that remain essentially mural and display all the difficulties mentioned earlier, that arise from beginning with a regulation field which then is broken by holes or by the addition of foreign matter to the surface. The now objectlike area is simply increased in scale until it is large enough to dwarf a man. Often it substitutes for the wall. By its sheer breadth the "object" reverts to a quasi field again (though not exactly a painting), for one's eyes and arms cannot possibly embrace the whole at once while standing at the usual distance of a half-dozen feet. A broken surface thus becomes a sort of topography relief in which one could travel, as though up and down the face of a cliff; and it also succeeds only partially in questioning the domination of the architectural setting, since fundamentally it needs the wall in one way or another. My own *Wall* (pl. 37) is a case in point.

Another group of works, such as those by Jean Follett (pls. 2, 35, 62, 80), which also employ the basic rectangle of the canvas (or a related box), manifest a kind of primitive or "magical" tendency through the creation of images which have the feeling of fetishes—though we sense their sophisticated origin. But these fetishes do not function on or in their field as images within a space, that is, the object–ground relation is not present. Instead, the rectangle is the "aura" of the image; it is in fact the equivalent of a *mandorla* or a halo, and so here too we bypass pure painting.

Fetishes also exist completely in the round. And frequently they are surrounded by other separated parts so that the larger arrangement causes one to think of shrines—not any specific one or belonging to any actual institution or religion—but a simile at least, a shrine to the self, emitting waves of "revelation." Some works which Jim Dine and Robert Rauschenberg have created in this vein (pls. 17, 106) come to mind.

Yet we must not suppose that these works look like a witch doctor's magic stick or like the plaster madonna-with-roses-and-lights that appears on so many of our lawns. Sometimes simple imagery of sorts can be made out, though often it slips out of focus as quickly as it is seized upon; occasionally it bursts blatantly forth out of the nameless sludge and whirl of urban events, precisely where and when it is least expected. In fact, much of this is eminently an art of the city, and if it comes from within, the dreams of the inner man are now closely bound up with some real enough pattern perceived in the externals of the streets.

Naturally, at this point the last vestiges of picture making have fallen away. The work begins to actively engulf the air around it, giving it shape, dividing it into parts, weighing it, allowing it to interact with the solids at such a rate or in such a strange manner that one now cannot help noticing the shape and feel of the gallery which, like some radar signal, sends back its shape to contend with the work of art. Here is where the two structures become inimical.

The shrine may expand to larger proportions, thus becoming a chapel or grotto. This was true of my earlier work (pls. 91, 92) and applies to Yayoi Kusama (pl. 49) and to the interior of Clarence Schmidt's large work (pls. 63–65). In some cases this happens as a consequence of a certain frustration caused by the discrepancy between the art and the surrounding architectural space—as though sheer size could drown out the discomfort. In others it is simply a turning away from this rift as an insoluble problem and a pursuit of the inner evolution of one's work, in which one thing suggests another, which in turn suggests another, and so on ... expanding the work until it fills an entire space or evolves one, thus becoming an Environment.

If Jackson Pollock spoke of being in his work while he painted (pls. 8, 111), it was true in so far as he stood amongst the pools of paint he had just poured, while others were being formed as he moved about. With a little work a spectator before the finished painting could *feel into* the same state of immersion. But in the case of Environments there is no question that one is inside and, for better or worse, a real part of the whole.

One stage of the journey from painting to Environment was now complete, and an almost logical progress can be observed if we glance again at the future implied by the collages of the Cubists. With the breakdown of the classical harmonies following the introduction of "irrational" or nonharmonic juxtapositions, the Cubists tacitly opened up a path to infinity. Once foreign matter was introduced into the picture in the form of paper, it was only a matter of time before everything else foreign to paint and canvas would be allowed to get into the creative act, including real space. Simplifying the history of the ensuing evolution into a flashback, this is what happened: the pieces of paper curled up off the canvas, were removed from the surface to exist on their own, became more solid as they grew into other materials and, reaching out further into the room, finally filled it entirely. Suddenly, there were jungles, crowded streets, littered alleys, dream spaces of science fiction, rooms of madness, and junk-filled attics of the mind. . . .

Inasmuch as people visiting such Environments are moving, colored shapes too, and were counted "in," mechanically moving parts could be added, and parts of the created surroundings could then be rearranged like furniture at the artist's and visitors' discretion. And, logically, since the visitor could and did speak, sound and speech, mechanical and recorded, were also soon to be in order. Odors followed.

The foregoing may give the impression that the modern art we are discussing is primarily concerned with an evolution of forms, such as the Cubist painters felt theirs was. This is partly true, but I think it is the particulars, the *"what"* of this art, that we may find more revealing and new. The *"what"* may also help explain the forms. As outlined earlier, we find a certain large range of objects and materials employed. They are not, however, indifferently chosen, but represent a recurrent class of things: memoirs, objects of everyday usage, industrial waste, and so forth. These firstly represent a further enlargement of the domain of art's subject matter, for in many cases these materials *are* the subject matter as well as the media; unlike the more neutral substance of paint, they refer directly to specific aspects of our lives. Coming from factories, the street, the household, the hardware store, dump, or garbage can, they force into focus once again the eternal problems of what may be (or become) art and what may not. The intellectuals' typical disdain for popular culture, for the objects and debris of mass production which appear abundantly in this work, is, as always, a clear instance of aesthetic discrimination: *this* is fit for art, *that* is not. Such high-mindedness is not at all different from the seventeenth century's belief in the greater value of "noble" themes over genre ones. Thus, attentiveness to the meaning of the materials chosen is essential.

Secondly, these materials practically guarantee a new range of forms not possible with conventional means. In fact, one can hardly avoid these fresh potentials. While it is true that many artists become frightened by them and tend to sugar-coat everything by recasting it in older molds, the plain fact must stare at one that when a piece of hardware is juxtaposed to some excelsior, and this in turn is placed upon a crumpled rag, a series of abrupt shifts occur with the passage of the eye (and of the touch) that simply are not found in the most highly contrast-full paintings. For in the latter, no matter what may be the shapes and colors, the medium of paint offers a sensible unity in which all other differences may take place. Hence the organization of an Assemblage or Environment poses difficulties hitherto rarely encountered, but they *can* be solved by accepting the nature of the materials employed rather than smoothing them over in order that they appear like a painting or memento in the most acceptable styles.

The third point is that the materials found in Assemblages and Environments are very often of the greatest physical fragility. In an increasing number of instances the work is intended to last only a short time and is destroyed immediately after exhibition. In nearly all, if their obsolescence is not deliberately planned, it is expected. And it is over this point that the greatest fear and hostility are voiced. Here is the central expression of this art's difference from the past. Why, people ask, if it is claimed to be art, will it not last? Why should one pay for "that"? The issue is not new, but the present work faces it head on more openly than it has been faced before.

Actually, the whole question of the enduring versus the passing has been coming up continually since Impressionism challenged the West's deep belief in the stable, clear, and permanent. These qualities were thought to be the high achievements of a striving, rational mind which has overcome brute and chaotic forces of nature. But while Impressionist paintings certainly conveyed philosophically the concept of the fleeting and changeful as a supreme value, the actual painting could be expected to last indefinitely. Yet, since the first decade of this century, pictures and constructions have more and more exhibited a short life span, betraying within a few years, or even months, signs of decay and (to the restorer) "faulty" technique. This has hardly been indifference on the part of the artist, though some have worried over it. It became necessary as means were sought to adequately embody those subtle and spontaneous feelings and responses that were the living expression of change.

Today, in the case of the most forward-looking Assemblages and Environments, the use of obviously perishable media such as newspaper, string, adhesive tape, growing grass, or real food points to a quite clearheaded decision to abandon craftsmanship and permanence (associated in the past with Art), for no one can mistake the fact that the work will pass into dust or garbage quickly. As the art critic Lawrence Alloway has observed, our "throwaway" culture has permeated deeply into the very methods and substance of contemporary creative art. (But, unlike our standardized products that are also made to be discarded, the art work is unique and personal.)

If change is to be lived and felt deeply, then the art work must be free to articulate this on levels beyond the conceptual. There is no fundamental reason why it should be a fixed, enduring object to be placed in a locked case. The spirit does not require the proofs of the embalmer. If one cannot pass this work on to his children in the form of a piece of "property," the attitudes and values it embodies surely can be transmitted. And like so many quite acceptable but passing facets of our lives, this art can be considered as a semi-intangible entity, something to be renewed in different forms like fine cooking or the seasonal changes, which we do not put into our pockets, but need nevertheless.

Change, governing both reality and art, has extended, therefore, from the expression of an idea arrested in a painting, to a work in which the usually slow mutations wrought by nature are quickened and literally made part of the experience of it; they manifest the very processes of creation–decay–creation almost as one watches. The use of debris, waste products, or very impermanent substances like toilet paper or bread, has, of course, a clear range of allusions with obvious sociological implications, the simplest being the artist's positive involvement, on the one hand with an everyday world, and on the other with a group of objects which, being expendable, might suggest that corresponding lack of status which is supposed to be the fate of anything creative today. These choices must not be ignored, for they reveal what in our surroundings charges the imagination as well as what is most human in our art. But beyond this is the larger issue of reality understood as *constant metamorphosis*. This viewpoint, this metaphysics, is more fundamental than our "throwaway" culture. The latter is the topical vehicle for the former and, while important, should become something else in time. The conception of a non-fixed, organic universe, however, has pervaded our thinking for a longer historical space. It lies, I am convinced, at the root of our present innovations, and is pointing straight ahead along this road for the near future.

Change—we may capitalize it in this context—suggests a form-principle for an art which is never finished, whose parts are detachable, alterable, and re-arrangeable in theoretically large numbers of ways without in the least hurting the work. Indeed, such changes actually fulfill the art's function.

Clarence Schmidt, for example, has reportedly worked for over thirty years on a mountaintop Environment near Woodstock, N.Y. He began by carving out along several acres, now mostly overgrown, rough-hewn rock terraces where he had originally conceived gardens. At present there remain obscured bridges, intimate clearings, winding paths looking out here and there over a large reservoir, and perhaps an isolated seat or two chipped into the rocky shale. Occasionally one stumbles across large cryptlike holes and curious piles and cones of layered stone with odd projections sticking out from their sides.

At the same time he dug into the face of the cliff and there built a number of strangely shaped rooms and passages, in which he lived. Gradually he added to them, room after room, until now they seem uncountable (a reasonable estimate establishes at least thirty-five). Their walls and ceilings are faced with bark and rough-cut boards picked up at the local lumber mill, and the outer rooms project fantastically over the cliffside in an array of differently-angled windows that offer a marvelous view. The inner areas are completely sealed except for a few light-wells that are so arranged as to permit just a bit of the day to enter, but no view of the sky. Architecturally, the spaces seem to have no conscious quality of "arrangement," or at least it is not a "rational" order. The space is slowly continuous and unwinding, rather than crisply delimited as in the usual house.

The rooms are filled with a stupefying richness of Christmas lights, dried ferns, silvered hemlocks, and artificial flowers that ornament tiny cubbyhole chapels and niches. Toys, stuffed animals and birds, old lamps, furniture—some of it built in—bric-a-brac, paintings by friends and visitors who have left them as presents, commercial signs, books, photos, and many other quasi-fetishistic objects are carefully set into these special places, and the whole effect is one of enchanted, baroque silence.

Up above, during the last four or five years, what was inside sprouted into a forest of tar-covered trees, truck tires, old beams, rowboats, farm implements, pillars of layered rock, and clusters of spiraling machine springs, all crisscrossed by multileveled pathways. Mirrors, ingeniously placed, abruptly confuse the space and add to the complexity that already issues from the masses of objects. There are more auto parts, dolls, bedsteads, television antennas, washing machines, fragments of building ornament, lawn sculptures, grass mowers, tangles of muffler tailpipes, hubcaps grouped like stars, venetian blinds splayed out in circular rays, and silver-foiled twigs resembling icicles against the blackened profusion. Again, artificial flowers abound and again, shrines—one of them to John F. Kennedy. In places the tar-smeared surfaces are painted over in silver, red, or blue, producing an ancient, crackled look. Poking out of this unbelievable agglomeration are the crazy-quilt tops of Schmidt's upper rooms. And on these as well as in other odd places, real bushes and flowers grow as counterparts to the dried and false ones underground, in turn relating to the natural terrain.

There is no end to the work, quite patently. Parts break and rot, the artist's thoughts about a particular project are revised or abandoned but, he tells us, it often turns out better that way, and it keeps him going. Though Schmidt is in his mid-sixties, he intends to work on for the rest of his years.

Schmidt's work, inviolate itself, contains useful lessons that may be applied differently by others. This kind of transforming and extending art can be made to be continued indefinitely by many artists, either according to a pre-fixed plan or on an individual basis, long after an initiator has stopped or died.

In the context, the weather should not be overlooked as an additional participant. Heat, wind, and rain will do more than merely reduce the materials to decay. Water might be channeled to flow through various parts, depending upon precipitation, and in turn affect other parts. Heat could inflate giant balloons and close electrical circuits controlling lights and sounds. Winds could shake suspended barrels, cadaverlike puppets, tree constructions, air horns, and junk metal, in the same spirit as the ancient oriental wind gongs. The weight of snow and ice might shift the delicate balances of any of these and set off a whole chain of occurrences. Using the principles of the landscape architect and gardener, flowers, shrubs, and trees could be arranged to bloom and turn color with prescribed regularity. The noise of rain and the wind swinging through the branches, the clanging of the constructions, cries of birds, and rasping of crickets —all could be picked up by tiny microphones and amplified earsplittingly over hidden loudspeakers. . . .

What this means is that the artist need not be the only one responsible for a creative action. While he may decide that only he can alter a piece as he sees fit during a period of time, he may also see a value in having nature or other artists, with their different backgrounds and tastes, contribute to its changes afterward. Using an extreme logic, this could imply that anything may be art and anyone may be an artist, but in plain fact it only extends the right of sensitive perception and creative activity to those who wish to respond appropriately, and artists usually proffer this invitation with discretion.

The problem posed here is a challenging one and, thus far, is the most tentatively approached. Whereas formerly the unique art work induced a related state of mind in the observer, the process is almost reversed in a few extreme cases (a serious application of the story of the Emperor's New Clothes). Marcel Duchamp conceived his Ready-Mades in something of this spirit and so, probably, did John Cage in his piece of "silence" entitled "Four Minutes and Thirty-Three Seconds," during which a pianist sat at a piano and only opened and closed the keyboard cover at prescribed intervals within the allotted time of the piece. Rauschenberg achieved the same effect with his series of blank canvases, and George Brecht currently arranges an event by sending small cards to his friends with a few words neatly printed on them, for example:

THREE LAMP EVENTS

● on.
off.

● lamp

● off.   on.

The work of art must now receive its meaning and qualities from the unique, expectant (and often anxious) focus of the observer, listener, or intellectual participant. But in a greater number of cases the responsibilities have at least been reapportioned to include certain outsiders who may or may not be told beforehand exactly what their duties are. The artist and his artist-public are expected to carry on a dialogue on a mutual plane, through a medium which is insufficient alone and in some instances is nonexistent before this dialogue, but which is given life by the parties involved.

One can go a step further. In utilizing variables more than any art has done for a long time, if ever before, this art must take into account the frequent product of variables: the accidental. Accident, as a trigger of the unconscious and, occasionally, of real freedom, is a common enough feature in much of the art of the twentieth century—but within limits. In current art it looms very large. An artist ostensibly involved with Change may actually be tangling with Chance. Change is closely bound up with Chance but it is not the same thing; for while Chance may palpably reveal some aspect of Change, the latter may also be regularized to exclude the former. If employing Change in one's work is risky at this time because of a probable high percentage of artistic failure due to nothing more than a lack of cooperation from a public invited to participate in the activity of transformation, a conscious use of Chance bypasses failure by building non-control into the work as a desideratum. Whatever happens by definition happens as it should. Theoretically, every occurrence is as "good" as every other.

Chance technique has a number of clear applications, which we shall illustrate. But before doing so, I should place them in perspective within this essay. In the foregoing, organicist principles have been primary. In the uses to which Chance has been put, the analytic tradition characteristic of Western thinking since the Greeks seems to govern its methodology. Art is broken down into basic elements or universals which are believed to hold true for all time. There are hues, shapes, positions, movements from one position to another; sounds in which may be distinguished amplitude, frequency, duration, timbre, attack–decay and where in space they originate; there are heat and cold by degrees, and kinds of touch

174

from rough to smooth; there are also the specific materials comprising these, the relationships between them and, finally, certain very basic meanings that are evoked by them according to cultural training.

Such categorizing may seem antithetical to an ongoing, extensional point of view, and one temperamentally inclined to the latter may be averse to it. Clearly, these categories have been at the heart of all the form–content, ego–society, body–soul conflicts that have filtered from the past to our day. Yet in the present case, if we *assume* that all the elements have an equal status, whether or not we actually believe this, then the chance operations (John Cage's expression for techniques designed to produce an indeterminate situation in music) applied to the above elements, if followed diligently, appear to have been able to provide a result close in spirit to the values espoused in the foregoing. The product is something which appears to be on its own, whole and separated from our anxieties, to be brought back into contact with us as though for the first time.

This is the only reason for using highly procedural techniques. It is paradoxical that to achieve a wholeness, self-evident and easy in its being, complicated and apparently unnatural means are sometimes necessary. If chance operations were merely an ingenious way of atomizing art into even more categories than history has accustomed us to, there would be no reason to discuss them. That they have in fact been liberating compels us to understand their use.

Chance, then, is meant to be a purposive following of rules, whereas Change is the following of intuition and wisdom. The rules of Chance are external to persons and history, while Change (even systemized into rules derived from, say, the Chinese *I Ching: The Book of Changes*) is dependent upon human experience. Chance operations are means to an end in which they are not necessarily inherent, but Change operations reflect a view of nature held by the artist, and as such are revealed in the transformations of the art.

Chance may be applied broadly to four areas comparable to Aristotle's "four causes": the efficient, material, formal, and final causes required of any being. The four areas are: the creator or creators (including nature as a creator), the materials used (including their life expectancy), the form that the work shall have (including its scale), and its function or purpose in life. As for the last, in most cases the implicit purpose will be an art work constructed for someone's perusal, but we shall have something more to say about this shortly. The other three can be discussed in order.

THE CREATOR(S) The artist determines, by roulette wheel or dice throws, how many persons in addition to himself will be part of the compositional activity. The maximum number is fixed in the beginning by how many persons are actually available for the work. Nature, as a co-creator, may be included or not by the fall of a coin: heads it is in; tails it is out. Nature's role will in any case depend on practical considerations, namely, the particular locale, the weather conditions, and the plant- and wildlife prevalent there. Nature cannot be asked, even by the roulette wheel, to furnish icy blasts at the Equator. Taking advantage of what *is* possible, it is not hard to imagine a rain storm making a marvelously soggy shapeliness of blotters, rags, and papers composed within an apple grove laden with ripe fruit. Long-term changes, only approximately foreseeable, can be brought about by insects, rotting, heat and cold, seeds dropped by birds and blown by winds, and so forth. Here again, duration in its protracted form becomes as much an uncertainty as physical constitution and appearance. Nature invited as a chance process could produce a painting on the ground merely by dropping leaves; passing cloudscapes could be viewed through plastic film or other structures built against the sky; rabbits and similar garden foes could eat their way right into a masterpiece if it seemed like a vegetable patch to them. . . . Finally, having allowed for nature's proclivities, each human creator is assigned a number within the total number of potential collaborators. Besides the initial artist, further turns of the roulette wheel decide exactly who shall execute the work, and when.

THE MATERIALS Materials may be obtained by cutting up all the items listed in a random selection of pages from the telephone company's "Yellow Pages." These are stirred into a pot and are picked out one after the other, blindfold, up to that number fixed by a previous chance operation. *Clothes, gas, spiderwebs, sky, river,* and *boxes* are examples. While I alone have just derived these as though in preparation for a work, this may be done by more than one person. The only limit to observe is, once again, the practicability of any choice. If the selection includes twenty tons of gold dust or three hermaphrodites with red hair, it may be quite difficult to come by them, and so in such instances, one must pick some more slips of paper from the pot.

Nature as a source of relatively inert materials—such as tree stumps, dirt, and rocks—rather than as an active agent of events, can be part of one's list, but on its own terms. If rocks and dirt are not readily available, then the creator(s) should go to where they are normally found: the country. The advantage is that an Environment (or Assemblage) can be constructed anywhere in the world without restriction to conventional exhibition places.

Furthermore, the life span of natural materials will decide the life span of the Environment just as much as nature's more palpable movements will decide it. (Here the materials as subject matter function also as quasi creators and the line between the categories blurs. But as we have seen, this is true for any organically conceived art.) If, on the other hand, chance moves decide that the work should be destroyed earlier, this must be done; if a longer life is called for— say, a continuous supply of green pine needles—then replenishing the perishables is in order.

COMPOSITION The ways in which the materials may be arranged can be spelled out for each material: in pattern (A), casually juxtaposed (B), or blended (C). In the previous section, six materials were listed. That means that each would be written as 1A, 1B, or 1C; 2A, 2B, or 2C, and so on. How many times each material is to be treated as A, B, or C will have been previously established by turns of the roulette wheel, throws of the dice, or other equivalent methods. Let us say there are twenty moves for *clothes,* seventeen for *gas,* two hundred and eleven for *spiderwebs,* three for *river,* none for *sky,* and fourteen for *boxes.* Six graphs are drawn on large sheets of paper and the proper number of A, B, or C treatments for each of the six materials are indicated thereon by corresponding squares. The graphs are put face up on the floor and a coin is tossed, without particular aim, onto each graph the appropriate number of times, to decide in what sequence each material is to be manipulated. These moves are listed on a sheet of paper. Then the six lists are combined by further chance operations on a single list in order to tell how, say, *boxes* are to be combined with some other material(s). Now the second material(s) is listed without a qualifying letter A, B, or C, because the first material already tells what is to be done with it. If it comes out that *boxes* (6) are to be arranged in pattern A with *river* (5), then we do not yet know exactly how to do this. For this information another list is compiled by the same chance methods, to tell specifically how the materials are to be arranged in pattern, casually juxtaposed, or blended with respect to each of the six materials' very considerable number of possible combinations. Now, the instruction for the compound *boxes* (A) *river* might specify:

> Ten suspended boxes of river water are clustered above eighteen boxes half-submerged in the river just offshore. The space between the boxes above and below, and between each other, will be twice the measurement of the largest member of each.

There are now two more times for the *boxes* to interact with the *river*, as determined earlier; but the *boxes* have eleven more times to interact with the other materials. Toward the end of the preparations, it may be that not all of a material's possible combinations are used up. At such a point the creator or creators simply stop and go on to the remaining materials, until all the possibilities are exhausted. The Environment is then executed according to plan. The scale of the work, large or small, is thus automatically decided.

The methods described above have hardly been precise; plenty of margin for the exercise of personal whim was left in the details. Moreover, in all cases the initiating artist remained essentially at the controls, either exclusively or as co-creator and, thereafter, as overseer. Some artists, however, may wish to be more disciplined. They may wish to subdivide the categories into many more parts and tighten up the whole process of chance operations by analyzing the controls, so that the last shred of artistic bias and mere habit will be eliminated and the unforseeable made more likely.

The artist can determine (1) that the decision as to whether a work of art shall be made or not is left to chance; (2) whether or not the initial artist shall execute it at all; (3) who, if anyone, shall be involved with it thereafter; (4) whether or not it shall be designated as art in fact, that is, whether it should not be called a dry-goods store, for instance, and opened for regular business.

At this point the "artist" as such is no longer a real entity. He has eliminated himself (and for one who has genuinely concerned himself with self-renunciation, the decision to do so must be respected). But its great poignancy is that it can never be a total act, for others must be made aware of the artist's disavowal of authorship if its meaning is not to be lost. It is just this which has been the dramatic lesson of the "inactivity" of Marcel Duchamp. And it is the lesson of monastic life in general. This is the threshold upon which aesthetics, ethics, religion, and life per se become indistinguishable. It is probably at the center of ultimate philosophy, and to that extent goes beyond the proper subject of this book, which has to do with *making* something.

But in so far as all art is, by implication, a discrimination of some values over others, it becomes the equivalent of philosophical activity. And thus the threshold must not be lost sight of. Any artist working with the main issues of current art must see it clearly. It is essential to know what Change and Chance are, where the one leaves off and the other begins, when to use one, when the other, and when neither; and it is most essential to know that the use of Chance can become a vehicle for the *denial* of art and self, as much as for their realization.

In any case, using Chance is a personal act no matter how much it attempts to be otherwise, for *a priori,* it is used, not simply given in to. Used responsibly, that is to say, with the artist acting as censor when an impossible or impractical instruction turns up and, above all, staying awake to what is taking place, the results can often be astonishing. Used stupidly, Chance will reduce to another confining academism. After all the shock of playing around with chance operations wears off, they seem much like using an electronic computer: the answers are always dependent on what information and biases are fed into the system in the first place. If dullness is built in, the chances are that dullness will come out. John Cage, who is chiefly responsible for making available to other artists the values and techniques of Chance in art, has gone to elaborate lengths to allow such methods to separate his and others' tastes from the music produced—to make it, in short, indeterminate. Yet the music is always recognizably Cage and often of very high quality. Others, imitating his approach, sound exactly like imitators and their work is dead, while still a few others, using the methods in their own way (and sometimes to the displeasure of Cage), make music which is live and obviously individual.

Hence, as a point of view and a technique, chance methodology is not only refreshing in the best sense of the word; it is extremely useful in dispersing and breaking up knots of "knowables," of groupings, relationships, and larger structures which have become obsolete and habitual through overuse. Everything, the stuff of art, of daily life, the working of one's mind, gets thrown into sudden and startling patterns, so that if old values are destroyed, new experiences are revealed. Chance, therefore, is a dramatic affair involving both our need for security and our need for discovery or risk.

All that we have discussed has taken place, with varying degrees of success. For however compelling this new direction of art, in actual practice its implications are only partly realized. Most artists involved cannot bring themselves to face the spatial (i.e. environmental) problem that introduced this book: the discrepancy between the organic, unmeasurable and extensional character of the forms of the Assemblages and Environments, and the limiting rectangularity of the gallery architecture in which they are usually found. Their work, though interesting, is fundamentally conventional.

If Change is considered central to the life and mode of creation of these works, the box shape, the frame, does more than offer a stimulating contrast to it; it imposes a very powerful denial of Change on the whole set-up. I believe consistency here is crucial. This is most obvious with the Environments. Gallery-exhibited Environments almost invariably tend to be untouchable, static display pieces in conformity with the gallery tradition. All the marvelous potentials of transformation and interactivity between art, the public, and nature are out of the question. And even when a little of this is made possible, it is so tentative that the old habits of gallery-spectatorship preclude any vital response on the public's part, limit the work's duration to the standard three-week show, and do not prepare anyone for the idea that nature could ever be involved, much less welcomed.

The only fruitful direction to take is toward those areas of the everyday world which are less abstract, less boxlike, such as the out of doors, a street crossing, a machine factory, or the seaside. The forms and themes already present in these can indicate the idea of the art work and generate not only its outcome but a give-and-take between the artist and the physical world. It would also lessen the fixed aesthetic reactions evoked by any art gallery, which unconsciously influence the artist as much as the public. Needless to say, this holds *a fortiori* for museums.

The evolution of this art is bringing us to a quite different notion of what art is. With the emergence of the picture shop and museum in the last two centuries as a direct consequence of art's separation from society, art came to mean a dream world, cut off from real life and capable of only indirect reference to the existence most people knew. The gallery and museum crystallized this idea by insisting upon a "shshsh—don't touch" atmosphere. Traditionally, it is supposed that art is born entirely from the heart or head and is then brought, all shiny and finished, to the showplace. Now, however, it is less and less conceived that way and is instead drawing its substance, appearances, and enthusiasms from the common world as we know it; and this, without any doubt, is a hint of how vestigial the gallery–museum situation is. With such a form as the Environment it is patently absurd to conceive it in a studio and then try to fit it into an exhibition hall. And it is even more absurd to think that since the work looks better in the studio because it was conceived there, that is the best and only place for it. The romance of the atelier, like that of the gallery and museum, will probably disappear in time. But meanwhile, the rest of the world has become endlessly available.

THE EVENT

Environments are generally quiet situations, existing for one or for several persons to walk or crawl into, lie down, or sit in. One looks, sometimes listens, eats, drinks, or rearranges the elements as though moving household objects around. Other Environments ask that the visitor-participant recreate and continue the work's inherent processes. For human beings at least, all of these characteristics suggest a somewhat thoughtful and meditative demeanor.

Though the Environments are free with respect to media and appeals to the senses, the chief accents to date have been visual, tactile, and manipulative. Time (compared with space), sound (compared with tangible objects), and the physical presence of people (compared with the physical surroundings), tend to be subordinate elements. Suppose, however, one wanted to amplify the potentialities of these subordinates. The objective would be a unified field of components in which all were theoretically equivalent and sometimes exactly equal. It would require scoring the components more conscientiously into the work, giving people more responsibility, and the inanimate parts roles more in keeping with the whole. Time would be variously weighted, compressed, or drawn out, sounds would emerge forthrightly, and things would have to be set into greater motion. The event which has done this is increasingly called a "Happening."*

Fundamentally, Environments and Happenings are similar. They are the passive and active sides of a single coin, whose principle is *extension*. Thus an Environment is not *less* than a Happening. It is not a movie set which has not yet seen action (like the blank canvas-arena of the "action" painter). It is quite sufficient in its quieter mode even though, in the point of evolution, the Happening

* I doubt that this is a term acceptable to all artists. It was part of the title of a score included in the body of an article written in early 1959 for the Rutgers University *Anthologist* (vol. 30, no. 4). This was apparently circulated in New York City. In October of the same year, I presented *18 Happenings in Six Parts* at the Reuben Gallery, a loft on New York's lower Fourth Avenue (now an artist's studio). A number of artists picked up the word informally and the press then popularized it. I had no intention of naming an art form and for a while tried, unsuccessfully, to prevent its use.

grew out of it. I suspect that the differences will eventually blur and matter less.

For the present, however, a kaleidoscopic sampling of occurrences typical of Happenings might be the following. They represent no one performance; nor is it true to say that all Happenings feel as kaleidoscopic as this account (although the collage-assemblage method of juxtaposing events to each other prevails in most of them).

Everybody is at a train station. It's hot. There are lots of big cartons sitting all over the arcade. One by one they start to move, sliding and careening drunkenly in every direction, lunging into commuters and one another, accompanied by loud breathing sound over the public-address system. Now it's winter, and it's cold and dark, and all around, little blue lights go on and off at their own speed, while three large brown gunny-sack constructions drag an enormous pile of ice and stones over bumps, losing most of it, and blankets keep falling over everything from the ceiling. A hundred iron barrels and gallon wine jugs hanging on ropes swing back and forth, crashing like church bells, spewing glass all about. Suddenly, mushy shapes pop up from the floor and painters slash at curtains dripping with action. A wall of trees tied with colored rags advances on the crowd, scattering everybody, forcing them to leave. Eating is going on incessantly, eating and vomiting and eating and vomiting, all in relentless yellow. There are muslin telephone booths for all, with a record player or microphone that tunes everybody in on everybody else. Coughing, you breathe noxious fumes, or the smell of hospitals and lemon juice.

A nude girl runs after the racing pool of a searchlight and throws water into it. Slides and movies, projected in motion over walls and hurrying people, depict hamburgers: big ones, huge ones, red ones, skinny ones, flat ones, etc. You push things around like packing crates. Words rumble past, whispering dee-daaa, ba-ROOM, lovely, love me; shadows jiggle on screens, power saws and lawnmowers screech just like the subway at Union Square. Tin cans rattle, soaking rags slush, and you stand up to shout questions at shoeshine boys and old ladies. Long silences when nothing at all happens, when bang! there you are facing yourself in a mirror jammed at you. Listen. A cough from the alley. You giggle, talk to someone nonchalantly while eating strawberry jam sandwiches. . . . Electric fans start wafting breezes of "New-Car" smell past your nose as leaves bury heaps of a whining, burping, foul, pinky mess.

One Happening, an unperformed score of mine written in 1962, can be decribed briefly:

Long maze of wall-size mirrors (as at oldtime carneys). ROys of blinking yellow, blue, and white lights. Quiet neons. Everybody wanders aimlessly. Rubbish on floors of passageways. Five janitors come in with vacuum sweepers, sucking up debris. Crackling sounds. Janitors leave. From above, whistling of some sad pop tune like "Don't Play It No More." More debris is dropped into passages. Crackling sounds again. Janitors rush around handing out brooms and everybody sweeps. Lots of dust, coughs. Mirrors begin to sway and shake. Whistling continues as high whine enters louder and louder. Wheelbarrows and shovels rolled in. Frenzied loading of trash, much noise. Brooms are grabbed from people, are held up close to mirrors and examined. Fellow comes in with wide brush and pail of soapy water and wipes over reflections. Janitors sweep and shout at each other from different passageways, *but their words are backwards.* They yell louder and faster. Then work and noise wears out and finally stops, dust settles, cans of beer are brought in for everybody. Workmen take a swig, burp, and pour beer on the floor. They go. Dead silence. Three pneumatic triphammers are dragged in. Compressors start. Floor is drilled into, noise is deafening, mirrors shatter.

Although the Assemblages' and Environments' free style was directly carried into the Happenings, the use of standard performance conventions from the very start tended to truncate the implications of the art. The Happenings were presented to small, intimate gatherings of people in lofts, classrooms, gymnasiums, and some of the offbeat galleries, where a clearing was made for the activities. The watchers sat very close to what took place, with the artists and their friends acting along with assembled environmental constructions. The audience occasionally changed seats as in a game of musical chairs, turned around to see something behind it, or stood without seats in tight but informal clusters. Sometimes, too, the event moved in and amongst the crowd, which produced some movement on the latter's part. But, however flexible these techniques were in practice, there was always an audience in one (usually static) space and a show given in another.

This proved to be a serious drawback, in my opinion, to the plastic morphology of the works, for reasons parallel to those which make galleries inappropriate for Assemblages and Environments. But it was more dramatically evident. The rooms enframed the events, and the immemorial history of cultural expectations attached to theatrical productions crippled them. It was repeatedly clear with each Happening that in spite of the unique imagery and vitality of its impulse, the traditional staging, if it did not suggest a "crude" version of the avant-garde Theater of the Absurd, at least smacked of night club acts, side shows, cock fights and bunkhouse skits. Audiences seemed to catch these probably unintended allusions and so took the Happenings for charming diversions, but hardly for art or even purposive activity. Night club acts can of course be more than merely diverting, but their structure or "grammar" is usually hackneyed and, as such, is detrimental to experimentation and change.

Unfortunately, the fact that there was a tough nut to crack in the Happenings seems to have struck very few of its practitioners. Even today, the majority continues to popularize an art of "acts" which often is well-done enough but fulfills neither its implications nor strikes out in uncharted territory.

But for those who sensed what was at stake, the issues began to appear. It would take a number of years to work them out by trial and error, for there is sometimes, though not always, a great gap between theory and production. But gradually a number of rules-of-thumb could be listed:

(A) *The line between art and life should be kept as fluid, and perhaps indistinct, as possible*. The reciprocity between the man-made and the ready-made will be at its maximum potential this way. Something will always happen at this juncture, which, if it is not revelatory, will not be merely bad art—for no one can easily compare it with this or that accepted masterpiece. I would judge this a foundation upon which may be built the specific criteria of the Happenings, as well as the other styles treated in this book.

(B) *Therefore, the source of themes, materials, actions, and the relationships between them are to be derived from any place or period except from the arts, their derivatives, and their milieu.* When innovations are taking place it often becomes necessary for those involved to treat their tasks with considerable severity. In order to keep their eyes fixed solely upon the essential problem, they will decide that there are certain "don'ts" which, as self-imposed rules, they will obey unswervingly. Arnold Schoenberg felt he had to abolish tonality in music composition and, for him at least, this was made possible by his evolving the twelve-tone series technique. Later on his more academic followers showed that it was very easy to write traditional harmonies with that technique. But still later, John Cage could permit a C major triad to exist next to the sound of a buzz saw, because by then the triad was thought of differently—not as a musical necessity but as a sound as interesting as any other sound. This sort of freedom to accept all kinds of subject matter will probably be possible in the Happenings of the future, but I think not for now. Artistic attachments are still so many window dressings, unconsciously held on to to legitimize an art that otherwise might go unrecognized.

Thus it is not that the known arts are "bad" that causes me to say "Don't get near them"; it is that they contain highly sophisticated habits. By avoiding the artistic modes there is the good chance that a new language will develop that has its own standards. The Happening is conceived as an art, certainly, but this is for lack of a better word, or one that would not cause endless discussion. I, personally, would not care if it were called a sport. But if it is going to be thought of in the context of art and artists, then let it be a distinct art which finds its way into the art category by realizing its species outside of "culture." A United States Marine Corps manual on jungle-fighting tactics, a tour of a laboratory where polyethylene kidneys are made, the daily traffic jams on the Long Island Expressway, are more useful than Beethoven, Racine, or Michelangelo.

(C) *The performance of a Happening should take place over several widely spaced, sometimes moving and changing locales.* A single performance space tends toward the static and, more significantly, resembles conventional theater practice. It is also like painting, for safety's sake, only in the center of a canvas. Later on, when we are used to a fluid space as painting has been for almost a century, we can return to concentrated areas, because then they will not be considered exclusive. It is presently advantageous to experiment by gradually widening the distances between the events within a Happening. First along several points on a heavily trafficked avenue; then in several rooms and floors of an apartment house where some of the activities are out of touch with each other; then on more than one street; then in different but proximate cities; finally all around the globe. On the one hand, this will increase the tension between the parts, as a poet might by stretching the rhyme from two lines to ten. On the other, it permits the parts to exist more on their own, without the necessity of intensive coordination. Relationships cannot help being made and perceived in any human action, and here they may be of a new kind if tried-and-true methods are given up.

Even greater flexibility can be gotten by moving the locale itself. A Happening could be composed for a jetliner going from New York to Luxembourg with stopovers at Gander, Newfoundland, and Reykjavik, Iceland. Another Happening would take place up and down the elevators of five tall buildings in midtown Chicago.

The images in each situation can be quite disparate: a kitchen in Hoboken, a *pissoir* in Paris, a taxi garage in Leopoldville, and a bed in some small town in Turkey. Isolated points of contact may be maintained by telephone and letters, by a meeting on a highway, or by watching a certain television program at an appointed hour. Other parts of the work need only be related by theme, as when all locales perform an identical action which is disjoined in timing and space. But none of these planned ties are absolutely required, for preknowledge of the Happening's cluster of events by all participants will allow each one to make his own connections. This, however, is more the topic of form, and I shall speak further of this shortly.

(D) *Time, which follows closely on space considerations, should be variable and discontinuous.* It is only natural that if there are multiple spaces in which occurrences are scheduled, in sequence or even at random, time or "pacing" will acquire an order that is determined more by the character of movements within environments than by a fixed concept of regular development and conclusion. There need be no rhythmic coordination between the several parts of a Happening unless it is suggested by the event itself: such as when two persons must meet at a train departing at 5:47 P.M.

Above all, this is "real" or "experienced" time as distinct from conceptual time. If it conforms to the clock used in the Happening, as above, that is legitimate, but if it does not because a clock is not needed, that is equally legitimate. All of us know how, when we are busy, time accelerates, and how, conversely, when we are bored it can drag almost to a standstill. Real time is always connected with doing something, with an event of some kind, and so is bound up with things and spaces.

Imagine some evening when one has sat talking with friends, how as the conversation became reflective the pace slowed, pauses became longer, and the speakers "felt" not only heavier but their distances from one another increased proportionately, as though each were surrounded by great areas commensurate with the voyaging of his mind. Time retarded as space extended. Suddenly, from out on the street, through the open window a police car, siren whining, was heard speeding by, *its* space moving as the source of sound moved from somewhere to the right of the window to somewhere farther to the left. Yet it also came spilling into the slowly spreading vastness of the talkers' space, invading the transformed room, partly shattering it, sliding shockingly in and about its envelope, nearly displacing it. And as in those cases where sirens are only sounded at crowded street corners to warn pedestrians, the police car and its noise at once ceased and the capsule of time and space it had become vanished as abruptly as it made itself felt. Once more the protracted picking of one's way through the extended reaches of mind resumed as the group of friends continued speaking.

Feeling this, why shouldn't an artist program a Happening over the course of several days, months, or years, slipping it in and out of the performers' daily lives. There is nothing esoteric in such a proposition, and it may have the distinct advantage of bringing into focus those things one ordinarily does every day without paying attention—like brushing one's teeth.

On the other hand, leaving taste and preference aside and relying solely on chance operations, a completely unforeseen schedule of events could result, not merely in the preparation but in the actual performance; or a simultaneously performed single moment; or none at all. (As for the last, the act of finding this out would become, by default, the "Happening.")

But an endless activity could also be decided upon, which would apparently transcend palpable time—such as the slow decomposition of a mountain of sandstone. . . . In this spirit some artists are earnestly proposing a lifetime Happening equivalent to Clarence Schmidt's lifetime Environment.

The common function of these alternatives is to release an artist from conventional notions of a detached, closed arrangement of time–space. A picture, a piece of music, a poem, a drama, each confined within its respective frame, fixed number of measures, stanzas, and stages, however great they may be in their own right, simply will not allow for breaking the barrier between art and life. And this is what the objective is.

(E) *Happenings should be performed once only.* At least for the time being, this restriction hardly needs emphasis, since it is in most cases the only course possible. Whether due to chance, or to the lifespan of the materials (especially the perishable ones), or to the changeableness of the events, it is highly unlikely that a Happening of the type I am outlining could ever be repeated. Yet many of the Happenings have, in fact, been given four or five times, ostensibly to accommodate larger attendances, but this, I believe, was only a rationalization of the wish to hold on to theatrical customs. In my experience, I found the practice inadequate because I was always forced to do that which *could be repeated,* and had to discard countless situations which I felt were marvelous but performable only once. Aside from the fact that repetition is boring to a generation brought up on ideas of spontaneity and originality, to repeat a Happening at this time is to accede to a far more serious matter: compromise of the whole concept of Change. When the practical requirements of a situation serve only to kill what an artist has set out to do, then this is not a practical problem at all; one would be very practical to leave it for something else more liberating.

Nevertheless, there is a special instance of where more than one performance is entirely justified. This is the score or scenario which is designed to make every performance significantly different from the previous one. Superficially this has been true for the Happenings all along. Parts have been so roughly scored that there was bound to be some margin of imprecision from performance to performance. And, occasionally, sections of a work were left open for accidentals or improvisations. But since people are creatures of habit, performers always tended to fall into set patterns and stick to these no matter what leeway was given them in the original plan.

In the near future, plans may be developed which take their cue from games and athletics, where the regulations provide for a variety of moves that make the outcome always uncertain. A score might be written, so general in its instructions that it could be adapted to basic types of terrain such as oceans, woods, cities, farms; and to basic kinds of performers such as teenagers, old people, children, matrons, and so on, including insects, animals, and the weather. This could be printed and mail-ordered for use by anyone who wanted it. George Brecht has been interested in such possibilities for some time now. His sparse scores read like this:

DIRECTION

Arrange to observe a sign
indicating direction of travel.

- travel in the indicated direction

- travel in another direction

But so far they have been distributed to friends, who perform them at their discretion and without ceremony. Certainly they are aware of the philosophic allusions to Zen Buddhism, of the subtle wit and childlike simplicity of the activities indicated. Most of all, they are aware of the responsibility it places on the performer to make something of the situation or not. As we mentioned before in connection with another of Brecht's pieces, this implication is the most radical potential in all of the work discussed in this book. Beyond a small group of initiates, there are few who could appreciate the moral dignity of such scores, and fewer still who could derive pleasure from going ahead and doing them without self-consciousness. In the case of those Happenings with more detailed instructions or more expanded action, the artist must be present at every moment, directing and participating, for the tradition is too young for the complete stranger to know what to do with such plans if he got them.

(F) *It follows that audiences should be eliminated entirely.* All the elements—

people, space, the particular materials and character of the environment, time—can in this way be integrated. And the last shred of theatrical convention disappears. For anyone once involved in the painter's problem of unifying a field of divergent phenomena, a group of inactive people in the space of a Happening is just dead space. It is no different from a dead area of red paint on a canvas. Movements call up movements in response, whether on a canvas or in a Happening. A Happening with only an empathic response on the part of a seated audience is not a Happening but stage theater.

Then, on a human plane, to assemble people unprepared for an event and say that they are "participating" if apples are thrown at them or they are herded about is to ask very little of the whole notion of participation. Most of the time the response of such an audience is half-hearted or even reluctant, and sometimes the reaction is vicious and therefore destructive to the work (though I suspect that in numerous instances of violent reaction to such treatment it was caused by the latent sadism in the action, which they quite rightly resented). After a few years, in any case, "audience response" proves to be so predictably pure cliché that anyone serious about the problem should not tolerate it, any more than the painter should continue the use of dripped paint as a stamp of modernity when it has been adopted by every lampshade and Formica manufacturer in the country.

I think that it is a mark of mutual respect that all persons involved in a Happening be willing and committed participants who have a clear idea what they are to do. This is simply accomplished by writing out the scenario or score for all and discussing it thoroughly with them beforehand. In this respect it is not different from the preparations for a parade, a football match, a wedding, or religious service. It is not even different from a play. The one big difference is that while knowledge of the scheme is necessary, professional talent is not; the situations in a Happening are lifelike or, if they are unusual, are so rudimentary that professionalism is actually uncalled for. Actors are stage-trained and bring over habits from their art that are hard to shake off; the same is true of any other kind of showman or trained athlete. The best participants have been persons not normally engaged in art or performance, but who are moved to take part in an activity that is at once meaningful to them in its ideas yet natural in its methods.

There is an exception, however, to restricting the Happening to participants only. When a work is performed on a busy avenue, passers-by will ordinarily stop and watch, just as they might watch the demolition of a building. These are not theater-goers and their attention is only temporarily caught in the course of their normal affairs. They might stay, perhaps become involved in some unexpected way, or they will more likely move on after a few minutes. Such persons are authentic parts of the environment.

A variant of this is the person who is engaged unwittingly with a performer in some planned action: a butcher will sell certain meats to a customer-performer without realizing that he is a part of a piece having to do with purchasing, cooking, and eating meat.

Finally, there is this additional exception to the rule. A Happening may be scored for *just watching*. Persons will do nothing else. They will watch things, each other, possibly actions not performed by themselves, such as a bus stopping to pick up commuters. This would not take place in a theater or arena, but anywhere else. It could be an extremely meditative occupation when done devotedly; just "cute" when done indifferently. In a more physical mood, the idea of called-for watching could be contrasted with periods of action. Both normal tendencies to observe and act would now be engaged in a responsible way. At those moments of relative quiet the observer would hardly be a passive member of an audience; he would be closer to the role of a Greek chorus, without its specific meaning necessarily, but with its required place in the overall scheme. At other moments the active and observing roles would be exchanged, so that by reciprocation the whole meaning of watching would be altered, away from something like spoon-feeding, toward something purposive, possibly intense.

(G) *The composition of a Happening proceeds exactly as in Assemblage and Environments, that is, it is evolved as a collage of events in certain spans of time and in certain spaces.* When we think of "composition," it is important not to think of it as self-sufficient "form," as an arrangement as such, as an organizing activity in which the materials are taken for granted as a means toward an end that is greater than they are. This is much too Christian in the sense of the body being inferior to the soul. Rather, composition is understood as an operation dependent upon the materials (including people and nature) and phenomenally indistinct from them. Such materials and their associations and meanings, as I have pointed out, generate the relationships and the movements of the Happening, instead of the reverse. The adage that "form follows function" is still useful advice.

Otherwise, a sort of artistic schizophrenia can result if *any* subject matter and material is subjected to *any* interesting formal technique. It may be that some subjects, because of our familiarity with and wide use of them, allow for more alternatives of transformation and grouping than other subjects. An apple can be painted in the Neo-Classic, Realist, Impressionist, Expressionist, and Cubist styles and still be recognized as an apple, but an electron microscope cannot. The Impressionist mode, for instance, would blur it beyond recognition—and at that point the real subjects become light, optical sensation, and paint, and *not* the microscope.

Because the Happenings are occupied with relatively new (at least new for art) subject matter and materials, the stylistic conventions used by the other arts, or by such philosophical disciplines as logic, are best left alone. To illustrate why, several years ago I used serial methods related to Schoenberg's twelve-tone technique. A root-molecule of events was written down: "a jam sandwich being eaten in a dining room, a person laughing outside a window, and an alarm clock going off periodically in the bedroom." This was the basic cluster of situations that was to grow into the Happening. I next graphed rows of occurrences for the three elements in the cluster. The sandwich's paper wrapper was to be opened fast and closed noisily, or opened slowly and without noise; the sandwich was to be bitten into hard, put down on the table, chewed with gusto; the wrapper was to be crunched, flattened out; etc., etc., all within prescribed units of time.

The time units were derived by multiplying one second through nine seconds by the number three: 3, 6, 9, 12, 15, 18, 21, 24, 27. Nine seconds was the chosen maximum duration for any single occurrence, and twenty-seven was the maximum duration for any group or "chord" of occurrences—as when laughing overlapped the clock's sound and the sandwich activities. These durations were to be performed progressively and without repetition until the row was completed. The other two elements were graphed similarly. The rows were then exchanged, reversed, and run simultaneously backwards and forwards, as all three rows were performed together. This amplified the small durations into three larger structures based on the same module, and unified the whole piece. The total time was nine minutes, as the total maximum for one event was nine seconds.

I went further in a few other works and wrote out rows for the spacing of events, the manner in which movements were to be made, and the specific ways in which sounds were to be produced. I had in mind the very thorough way that the composer Karlheinz Stockhausen developed serialism, whereby all the elements of sound could be made mathematically consistent. But while this was possible in music, particularly electronic music, whose rudiments are relatively nonassociative, this was not possible with the materials of a Happening, with their high degree of everyday usage. And I did not want to lose all the advantages these provided by deliberately choosing more neutral events (about which I shall say more shortly). The worst difficulty to arise out of these procedures, however, was that as they became more exacting, performance became nearly impossible.

The results on paper were interesting enough, but in action (as far as any action was capable of being derived from the complicated scores) the effect was static and mechanical. The events were simply not eventful. A regimen unrelated to their natural qualities seemed to have been superimposed upon them. The scheme was self-evidently "formal" but the subject matter was not; or it had some as yet unrevealed form that was hidden because it was not respected. I concluded that to do this at all, limits had to be observed in choosing the initial stuff of the Happening. And these limits were contrary to the principal direction the art was taking.

We generally mean by "formal" art (the fugues of Bach, the sonnets of

Shakespeare, Cubist paintings) an art that is primarily manipulative. As in a chess game, the manipulation is intellectual, whereby elements of the work are moved according to strict, sometimes self-imposed regulations. The weaving of these elements into groupings, regroupings; the losing and finding of themes, sub-themes, and counterthemes, seemingly disparate yet always dominated by the relentless inevitability that they shall resolve at the end, is the peculiar fascination of such an art.

Formal art must be made of a substance that is at once stable and general in meanings. A formalist cannot easily use the horrifying records of Nazi torture chambers, but he can use a simple statement like "the sky is blue," abstract shapes such as circles and squares, the raising and lowering of an arm that does nothing else. The impact of the imagery, the "what," is not as important as the intricacy and subtlety of the moves the imagery is put through.

A formalist who wishes to make a Happening must choose with discretion situations that can be freely manipulated without jarring the overtones of the imagery within them. A group of men all in white doing calisthenics, a ticking metronome, a sheet of paper being moved variously across the floor are obviously easily formalized. But for this to become truly great, I think that some time must elapse. The media are still too undigested for us to feel at home with them. This is essential: to be profitably involved in an activity of arrangements, the materials arranged must not command attention. At present, the media are all rather unstable because their meanings in their new context tend to arise more quickly than anything else. Kleenex may be a commonplace, but collected in quantity in a Happening would immediately push into relief all that we have only half-consciously thought about Kleenex and its intimate uses.

Therefore, in making a Happening, it is better to approach composition without borrowed form theories, and instead to let the form emerge from what the materials can do. If a horse is part of a work, whatever a horse does gives the "form" to what he does in the Happening: trotting, standing, pulling a cart, eating, defecating, and so forth. If a factory of heavy machinery is chosen, then the clanging of motorized repetition might easily cause the form to be steadily repetitive. In this way a whole body of nonintellectualized, nonculturized experience is opened to the artist and he is free to use his mind anew in connecting things he did not consider before.

Think of the following items: tires, doughnuts, Cheerios cereal, Life Savers candy, life preservers, wedding rings, men's and women's belts, band saws, plastic pools, barrel hoops, curtain rings, Mason jar gaskets, hangman's nooses —one could go on almost indefinitely. They are all obviously united by a common circular shape (an observation that could be made by a botanist or a standard auto parts salesman as well as by any painter; for the recognition and use of physical resemblances is not the special talent of artists alone, even if the tradition of form analysis would seem to tell us so). By juxtaposing any half dozen of these items, an idea for a Happening could emerge. And from this combination, meanings not normally associated with such things could be derived by minds sensitive to symbols. Here is the score for an unperformed Happening I have written as an illustration:

Naked women eat giant bowls of Cheerios and milk atop a mountain of used tires. Children disgorge barrels of whitewash over the mountain. A hundred yards away, men and women swimmers in brightly colored plastic pools continually leap out of the water to catch with their mouths rubber gaskets festooned with Life Saver candies that hang from chains of men's belts. The mountain is taken down, tire by tire, and moved into the pools, and the water spills out. The children tie the adults together with the belts. They pour whitewash over the now still heaps of bodies. Then they buckle dozens more of the belts around their necks, waists, and legs. They take the remaining Life Savers to a factory-fresh tire shop and offer them for sale in laughy voices.

In performance, this would be first and foremost a rough, fast-moving affair. But on reflection, the overtones of salvation implicit in the Life Saver theme combine with the supposed nourishment of the cereal, the "pleasure of life" in the candies, the baptismal-sacrificial symbol of the whitewash (milk) bath and the bathing pools (where swimmers leap for Life Savers) and with the tire as the "wheel of progress and fortune." The "death" of this last object (it is *used,* i.e. useless) is built up by combination with others into a strong mound image, thus alluding to the phoenix idea of life-out-of-death. The mound is then destroyed as it is dumped, piecemeal, into the pools whose waters of life are displaced. The children, as direct regeneration images, leave the dying adults tied (united) in death by their belts, and carry on in gentle fun among the living in the brand-new tire shop.

The whole work has a humorous, almost slapstick immediacy about it, in spite of the underlying symbolism, because the imagery is drawn from daily life and juxtaposed in unexpected ways. Cheerios, Life Savers, and tires (which resemble life preservers) are an amusing group, whatever they reveal to depth psychology. Yet in composing it, I played around with the images on paper, shifting them this way and that, letting one thing suggest another, without the slightest thought about "meanings" per se. At the time I was only interested in a certain vividness.

Shifting things around can be an excellent mode of *performance* as much as of composition. Just as an Environment or an Assemblage can be maintained in prolonged transformation by allowing its parts to be rearranged in numbers of ways, the same can apply to a Happening. This would simply continue the compositional process into the performance process and the two usually distinct phases would begin to merge as the caesura between them is pulled out. Suppose, for example, that three environments and five actions are selected, partly by taste and partly by chance methods. The following score, also written to illustrate the text, shows what might result:

ACTIONS	ENVIRONMENTS AND TIMES
Spaghetti is cooked and eaten by at least two people	A Supermarket— Thursday, Friday, 9 A.M.
At least three motionless men are covered from head to toe, with chocolate icing, by at least the same number of women	

A group of at least fif-
teen dogs on leashes are
fed tinned dog food by
their masters

A Street—
Thursday, Friday,
5 P.M.

At least ten people are
packaged up in plastic
film and are dumped
or delivered by truck

A City Dump—
Thursday, Friday,
12 Noon

At least twenty people
with brooms sweep as
long as necessary

Each action may be performed once or twice, and at one or two prescribed environments and at their respective times, as desired.

At no time is it known if actions will be performed at all of the three environments, since the choice is left to the performers, nor what the number and kind of actions will be at the environments chosen. That is, it may be that all five actions will be performed at the supermarket at 9 A.M. on both Thursday and Friday. This would make quite a melange in that place and would leave the other two intentionally unused as a kind of psychological counterpoint. Perhaps the dog-feeding and the sweeping would occur together on the street, while the spaghetti and chocolate parts were taking place at the dump. Only the human packages would be delivered to the supermarket and put into shelves. Each group might then decide not to repeat its action and the Happening would be over. Or perhaps the package dumping and chocolate parts would be the only actions repeated the next day, this time on a busy street at 5 P.M. The ninety-six possible combinations are numerous and dramatic enough to make this small list of events both unexpected and sufficiently different in every case.

There are related ways of setting off rearrangements of fixed numbers of actions such as by *cueing,* in which performers are given a set of actions that are signaled, knowingly or unknowingly, by one another or by natural occurrences such as the sound of a car horn or a cloud formation. These cues also may be responded to in any one of a number of alternative ways in each instance, so here again the combinations are quite varied.

Finally, chance may determine nearly everything, and personal preference and the rumblings of the imagination will be put aside. I say chance operations may "nearly" determine everything, for any sensitive mind will tend to make connections between the actions which he finds occurring and those in which he is taking part, even if he had no way of knowing them beforehand. There are some artists, to be sure, who believe that the importance of the technique is to *disconnect* the moments of experience. They prefer to assume that no relationships need exist, that the events occur for and of themselves. It is possible that after long intellectual discipline a personality can erase its need for contingencies. This in itself is never complete, as I mentioned earlier, for it is an achievement, a state of blessedness in contrast to, and often expressed as in opposition to, the way everybody else thinks. However, I do not know of any artist who can say he has achieved even this, although the attempt is quite respectable. I doubt that any artist really wants to achieve this in our particular context, even when he speaks of "things for themselves." I sense, from such statements and from the art produced under this philosophy, much more a desire to become involved in the tangible world in a civilization whose thought and art has made this difficult. The advantage of chance methods, in my view, is that they free one from *customary* relationships rather than from any relationships. New ones will be noticed by the observant artist, whether he professes to like this or not. Most of the time he seems to like it.

The preceding discussion of composition has been a summary of all the rules-of-thumb raised respecting Happenings, rather than being merely technical. Problems of materials and content enter into the question at every stage and so I should like to re-emphasize the importance of a pervasive process which is manifestly organic and not divided into categories. Analytic writing, because of the very nature and history of the words we use, tends towards the broken-apart and divided and is necessary for the sake of convenience. But the only art that is so fractured is academic art, and thus I made it clear throughout the listing of the conditions I believe to be crucial to the Happening as an art, that they are not iron-clad rules but fruitful limits within which to work. As soon as they are found to be useless they will be broken, and other limits will take their place.

This short essay has been in one sense an account of an avant-garde. It has also been an analysis of a world view. It has proceeded on the assumption that at present any avant-garde art is primarily a philosophical quest and a finding of truths, rather than purely an aesthetic activity; for this latter is possible, if at all, only in a relatively stable age when most human beings can agree upon fundamental notions of the nature of the universe. If it is a truism that ours is a period of extraordinary and rapid change, with its attendant surprises and sufferings, it is no less true that in such a day all serious thought (discursive or otherwise) must try to find in it a pattern of sense. In its own fashion a truly modern art does just that.

Thus, for us now, the idea of a "perfect work of art" is not only irrelevant because we do not know what are the conditions for such a phantasm, but it is, if desired, presumptuous and unreal. Though great works are surely possible and may be looked forward to, it is in the sense that they may be moments of profound vision into the workings of things, an imitation of life, so to speak, rather than artistic tours de force, i.e., cosmetics.

I have focused upon this concept of the real, suggesting a course of action in art that is related to what is likely our experience today, as distinct from what are our habits from the past. I have considered important those aspects of art which have been consciously intended to replace habit with the spirit of exploration and experiment. If some of the past is still meaningful, as it assuredly is, then what is to be retained in the present work is not archaistic mannerisms, easily recognized and praised for this reason, but those qualities of personal dignity and freedom always championed in the West. In respecting these, the ideas of this book are deeply traditional.

42
HAPPENINGS

THE FOLLOWING is a selection of Happenings accompanied by illustrative photographs or diagrams whenever possible. There are a number of works by French, German, Czechoslovakian, and Japanese artists, to give some sense of the international scope of the art: Paris and Cologne are represented, respectively, by Jean-Jacques Lebel and Wolf Vostell. The activities of the Gutai Group of Osaka—Akira Kanayama, Sadamasa Motonaga, Shuzo Mukai, Saburo Murakami, Shozo Shimamoto, Kazuo Shiraga, Atsuko Tanaka, Tsuruko Yamasaki, and Michio Yoshihara—are described in brief notes by Jiro Yoshihara. To these are added photos of one of the Group's joint efforts, the *Sky Festival* of 1960, during which they and some non-Japanese artists flew paintings from a department store roof by gas-filled balloons. Next, there are further examples of George Brecht's brief scores, better known as "Events," which have been influential in professional circles and deserve a wider public. I also reproduce scores by Kenneth Dewey, who, though he has been working mainly in Europe during the last two years, developed independently in San Francisco. Czechoslovakia is represented by Milan Knížák and Soňa Svecová, members of the Art of the Actual group in Prague.

Finally, there are several by myself, to further document my application of the ideas expressed in the text. These should reveal the range of approaches to the Happening, and how much my own view, while it concurs in some ways, is biased in others. Most of us did not know of each other until recently; some of us still do not have any contact. In contrast to the increasingly homogenized character of the conventional forms of international creativity, the Happenings, I am glad to say, are distinct, both regionally and personally.

Excepting Brecht's pieces, I have omitted scenarios by my other New York colleagues whose works appear in the photographic section of the book, because a generous selection of them has already been published in Michael Kirby's *Happenings* (E. P. Dutton, New York, 1965). I thought that by avoiding repetition at this early stage, our two books could better complement one another.

JAPANESE OF THE
GUTAI GROUP

For the record, the dates accompanying these photographs seem to indicate the priority of the Japanese in the making of a Happening type performance. Even earlier in America, John Cage in 1952 organized an event at Black Mountain College combining paintings, dance, films, slides, recordings, radios, poetry, piano playing, and a lecture, with the audience in the middle of the activity. Since my own first efforts, in 1957, were done in Cage's composition class, where he described this event, I should mention it as an important catalyst. I had enrolled in the class to learn more about the sounds I was employing in my Environments at the time. And although, even then, I wanted as much as possible to avoid combining the arts, his 1952 example was an encouraging influence. Similarly influential were experiments by George Brecht, Al Hansen, Dick Higgins, and Jackson MacLow, who joined the class shortly thereafter. Of the Gutai's activities I knew nothing until Alfred Leslie mentioned them to me two years later, and it was not until late 1963 that I obtained the information presented here. This is a rare case of modern communications malfunctioning.

Above. SADAMASA MOTONAGA. [No note was provided for this work, but clearly, a very long balloon is being inflated. It emerges from a hole in a panel mounted on the stage, and as it extends out over the audience it emits smoke from tiny holes along its surface, perhaps deflating shortly afterwards—A. K.] From *Second Gutai Theater Art,* Sankei Hall, Osaka, April 1958.

Left. AKIRA KANAYAMA. "The enormous balloon became bigger and bigger on the stage, changing color, turning and swaying. At last Kanayama cut it right in two and it withered." From *First Gutai Theater Art,* Asahi Hall (?), Tokyo, and Sankei Hall, Osaka, May 1957.

Right. SHUZO MUKAI. "Mukai made a painting on the board and the faces."

214

Below. "At last he brought a man and placed him on the painting, then painted on his back and finished." From *Gutai Theater Art,* Sankei Hall, Osaka, November 1962.

SABURO MURAKAMI. "Murakami breaks the big paper screen with hands and a club." From *First Gutai Theater Art,* Asahi Hall (?), Tokyo, and Sankei Hall, Osaka, May 1957.

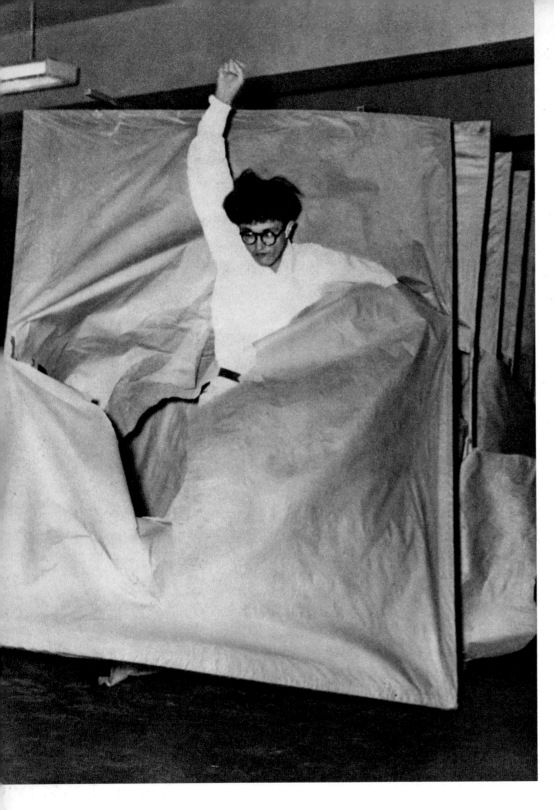

SABURO MURAKAMI. "Breaking through many paper screens." Ohara Hall, Tokyo, October 1955.

SHOZO SHIMAMOTO. "Shimamoto hit the end of the pipe hanging from a beam. Then thousands of ping pong balls came down on the stage." From *First Gutai Theater Art,* Asahi Hall (?), Tokyo, and Sankei Hall, Osaka, May 1957

KAZUO SHIRAGA. "Making a work with one's body. Material is mud." Outside (?) Ohara Hall, Tokyo, October 1955.

KAZUO SHIRAGA. "Attacking the red-painted logs with an ax." [Undoubtedly it was a question of striking as many of the logs as possible, swirling ferociously, before they came down upon the artist—A. K.] At Nishinomiya Beach, near Osaka, April 1956.

KAZUO SHIRAGA. "Some assistants shot arrows onto the screen, and Shiraga thrust in spears to complete it." From *First Gutai Theater Art,* Asahi Hall (?), Tokyo, and Sankei Hall, May 1957.

ATSUKO TANAKA. "Miss Tanaka is testing her theater costume of many electric bulbs." At her studio, April 1957.

Right. MICHIO YOSHIHARA. "The backdrop, costumes, and make-up are all white, except that each person has a red part. Only the red parts move, to Rock 'n Roll music." From *Gutai Theater Art,* Sankei Hall, Osaka, November 1962.

Below. TSURUKO YAMASAKI. "Performers hit, break by hammer, cut by drill, and make noise on the big circular panel of tin." From *Gutai Theater Art,* Sankei Hall, Osaka, November 1962.

SKY FESTIVAL. [A painting by New York painter Alfred Leslie is being sent aloft from the roof of the Takashimaya Department Store—A. K.]

Left.

SKY FESTIVAL. "Hung from balloons are enlarged paintings by Gutai members and famous artists outside of the group." *International Sky Festival,* performed by the Gutai Art Association on the rooftop of the Takashimaya Department Store, Osaka, April 1960.

Many of the following pictures
have no accompanying captions or notes,
as they are self-explanatory.

FUNERAL CEREMONY OF THE ANTI-PROCES

Performed in Venice on July 14, 1960.

A cocktail is served at the Palazzo Contarini-Corfù, home of the musician Frank Amey. About 150 people attend; they were asked to come in formal dress and to bring white flowers. At 6 P.M. they are ushered into a great, ancient funeral hall, at the center of which the body lies, covered with a gold-embroidered drape and flowers, and surrounded by lit church candles. The ceremony begins.

A man enters, his face under a black cape covering his eyes: the executioner. He kills the body with a large butcher's knife and as he does so, the choir of widows sings a hymn in Latin, cries, and screams. Then Lebel reads a violent page of the Marquis de Sade about death and love. Complete awed silence.

Then American poet Alan Ansen reads a few lines of Huysmans. Eulogy is ended while a man behind a small metal curtain masturbates. Others pray.

Then body is carried down steps of palace into the street by Amey, Ansen, and Lebel, people follow slowly. Outside, pedestrians take their hats off thinking it's a real funeral. Body is taken to awaiting gondolas, is put in front of first gondola covered with flowers. Other people take speedboats, about forty-five people board gondolas and slowly advance up Grand Canal. The boats make a circle. Hymns. Body is thrown into water (like in the navy), also flowers. It was a sculpture by Jean Tinguely. The Anti-Procès manifestation was dead and buried.

FOR EXORCISING THE SPIRIT OF CATASTROPHE

*Performed at the Raymond Cordier Gallery in Paris,
October 1962, and at the Boulogne Movie Studios in
a different, extended and developed form, February
1963.*

234 Environment of walls by Ferró, Kudo, Hiquely, Lebel, Lilian Lijn. Technical assistant, Alan Zion. Production by Titanus (MGM) Film (very corrupt, badly cut, poor commentary) later released under the title "Il Malamondo." Audience of about 120; length, an hour and a half.

Entrance of parade to jazz music. A large metal sculpture is beaten and broken. Two naked girls start large collage painting on wall. Lebel makes collage (with political headlines) on their bodies. They dance as they paint and glue, then they pass into international blood bath (bathtub full of chicken blood and water), put on masks of Kennedy and Krushchev (this was long before Dallas murder —no connection) and wash off headlines with blood, climb into hammock with third girl: sex.

Simultaneously, color slides of bodies and paintings are projected by Ferró onto the body of a woman's black silk underwear. Ferró afterwards paints a picture with electric drill, phallus sticking out from pants, dipped into girl. Kudo as sex priest makes silent sermon with immense papier-mâché phallus, then screams in Japanese, caresses public with the phallus, goes into mystic orgasm and then collapses.

A large head (over nine feet high) cries poems; wood, books, photographs, finally the body of a girl drop out of right eye like tears. Lebel as TV man hallucinates in electronic language, waving yin–yang code flags. (Political propaganda in electronic code.) Cans of paint are thrown by public onto board twirled very fast by a motor, while a machine paints a fine stripe of red on it. Two plainclothes policemen. They say nothing.

Jazz plays very fast, swinging stimulating sounds; a girl from the audience takes off her clothes and dances. Another one climbs into hammock with girl there. Lebel paints picture on transparent plastic and crashes it onto floor with girl. Ferró projects nudes onto public and onto belly of girl. Two men scream and kick photographer. Pot (marijuana) is sneaked into Cary Grant's dressing room behind set; Happening continues with improvisations for another thirty minutes until studio manager turns off lights. About twenty people follow cast and band into vast dressing rooms in basement. Orgy in showers. Everyone departs around 3 A.M.

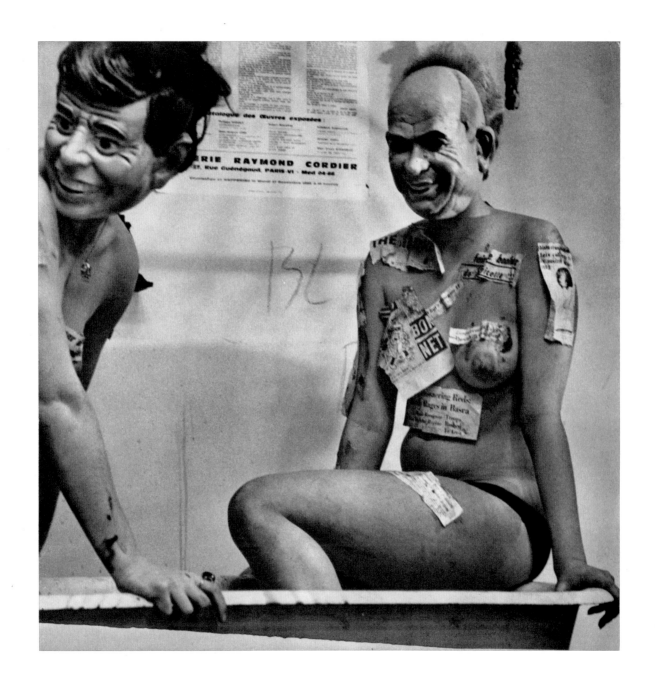

236

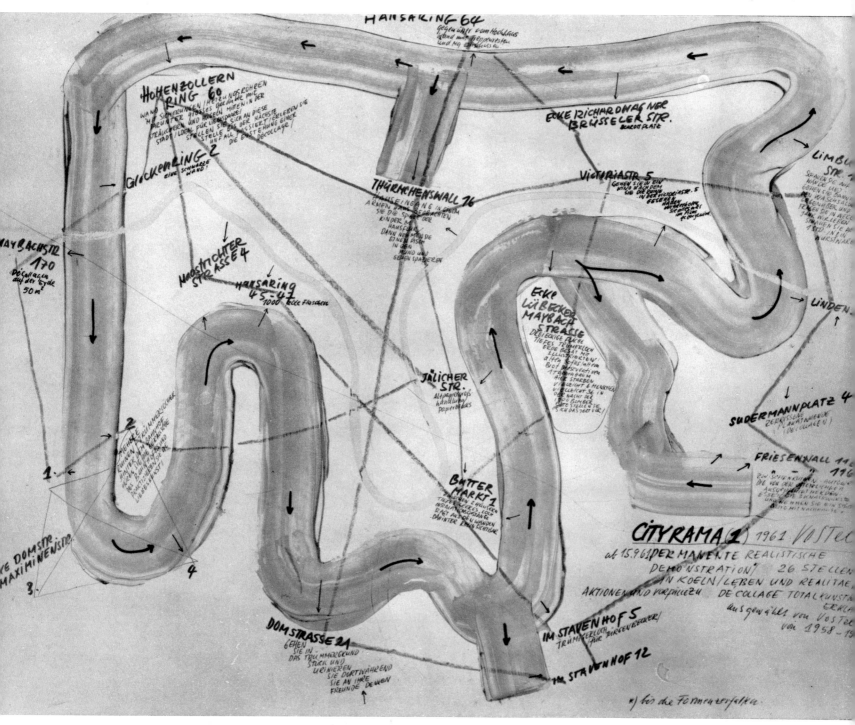

CITYRAMA 1

Performed September 15, 1961. A permanent, realistic demonstration in twenty-six places in Cologne. Life and reality, actions and events explained in the total art of décollage. Places selected by Vostell between 1958 and 1961.

go and see:
1) the ruins at maximinen street; entrance on dom street
2) the ruins at maximinen street; entrance on dom street
3) the ruins at maximinen street; entrance on dom street
4) the ruins at maximinen street; entrance on dom street

(several bomb-ruined houses—behind the main railway station—enter the ruins and listen to the sounds of the railway and practice the art of love)

5) sudermann place
6) maximinen street
7) dom street no. 21

(urinate in the bomb rubble and think of your best friends)

8) hohenzollern circle no. 60

(stand on the corner and wait for the next accident to happen)

9) in stavenhof street, next to no. 5 (for juergen becker)
10) corner of luebecker street and maybach street

(stand on the corner for about five minutes and ponder whether six or thirty-six human beings perished during the night of the thousand-bomber airraid)

11) linden street no. 58
12) thuermchenswall street no. 16 (doorway)

(go into this poor house and watch the games of the children—then put a fresh fish in your mouth and go for a stroll)

13) maastrichter street no. 4
14) maybach street no. 170
15) juelicher street no. 18
16) corner of richard wagner street and bruesseler street
17) stavenhof street, next to no. 12
18) friesenwall street nos. 116–118

(there are old car wrecks here, which the public dismantles—eat three knockwurst, then take a piece from the cars for yourself)

19) hansaring street nos. 45–47
20) friesenwall street nos. 112–116
21) friesenwall street nos. 112–116
22) buttermarket street no. 1 (opposite)
23) victoria street no. 5

(after you have seen the ruins, go to a movie in eigelstein street and mimic everything that is shown)

24) hansaring street no. 64
25) glockenring street no. 2
26) limburger street no. 15

(from here go to a laundromat and ask someone what year we are living in; gaze for one hour without interruption at the window display of a sausage shop)

(translated by Dorothy Schulz)

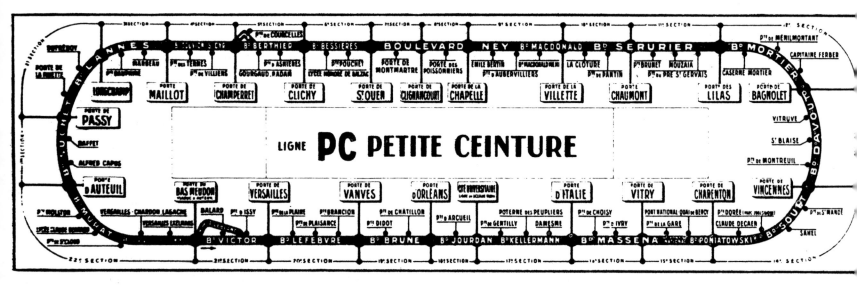

VOSTELL décollageur VOSTELL décollageur VOSTELL décollageur VOSTEL

vous envite mardi le 3 juillet	invites you to a „HAPPENING"	ladet Sie ein, Dienstag, den 3. Juli
à Paris de vivre un «HAPPENING»	on Tuesday, July 3. in Paris.	In Paris ein „HAPPENING" zu erleben.
Prenez l'autobus n'importe quelle	Just take a bus of the PC line	Nehmen Sie irgendwann den Autobus
heures - de la ligne PC **PETITE CEINTURE**	some time - Petite Ceinture	der Linie PC - Petite Ceinture
22 sections - 20 Boulevards.	22 line-sections - 20 boulevards.	22 Teilstrecken - 20 Boulevards. -
Allez autour de Paris	Drive around in Paris.	Fahren Sie um Paris herum
Faites attencion aux circonstances	Keep a look out for the acustic and at	Achten Sie auf die gleichzeitigen
accoustiques et optiques simultanées	the same time optical impressions.	akustischen und optischen Umstände. -
Bruits - Cris - Vois	Noise - cries - voices - walls with	Lärm - Schreie - Stimmen - Wände mit
Murs d'affiches (décollages)	placards torn or hanging down	abgerissenen Plakaten (décollagen) -
Décombres — Ruines etc.	(décollages) debris - ruins etc.	Trümmer - Ruinen - etc.

Announcement and plan for *Ligne Petite Ceinture*, 1962 (?)

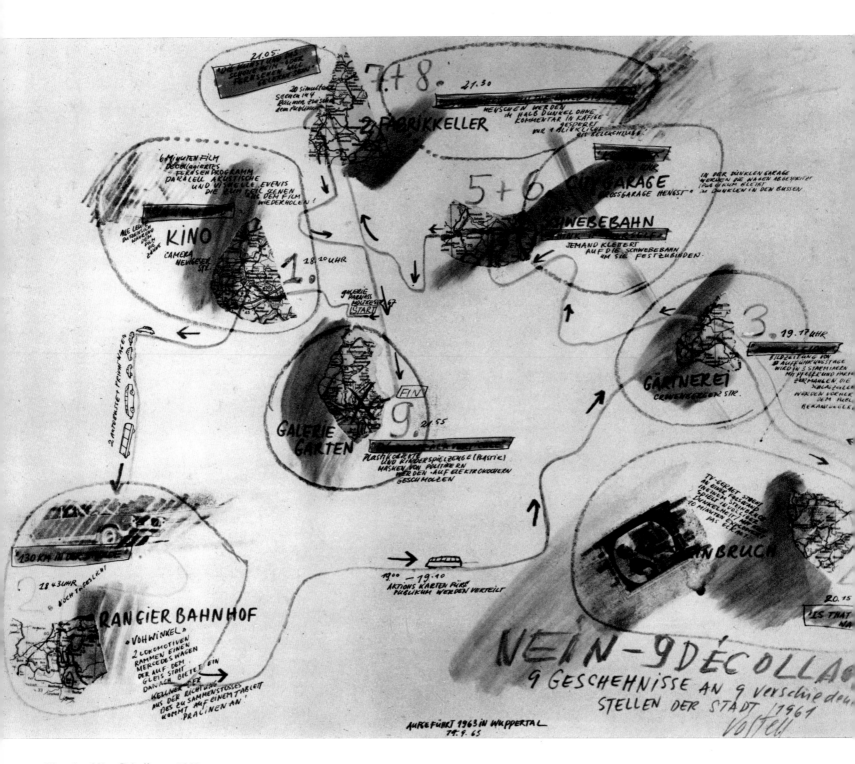

Plan for *Nine Décollages*, 1965

"NO": LIFE AS A PICTURE—A PICTURE AS LIFE: NINE DECOLLAGES

*Performed in Wuppertal, July 14, 1963, between 6
and 8 P.M. First printed in* Décollage *(ed. Vostell),
No. 4 (1964), Cologne.*

6:00 galerie parnass wuppertal 67 moltke street—
residential section

6:01 mr m wants to know whether his taking part
in the bus trip will

6:02 damage his reputation—inquisitive audience
rather restless

6:03 awaits a beginning—but the beginning

6:04 lies three months in the past at the time of the
preparations

6:05 police escort ready

6:06 director j of the gallery still not found

6:07 reporter b asks: mr vostell, what size shoe do
you wear?

6:08 someone is picking his nose

6:09 audience is loaded on the buses

6:10 leaves in the direction of nevigeser street
movie theater

6:11 b shows his picture postcards

6:12 v shoots his flashgun into the faces of the
people—do they have

6:13 a face? m sprays them with perfume

6:14 the audience coughs

6:15 b shows his picture postcards

6:16 v flashes

6:17 arrival at movie theater

6:18 owner of theater (with a worried look) asks:
are there only

6:19 juvenile delinquents coming?—audience sits
amidst

6:20 electronic flashers, searchlights, transistors—
the 6 min films

6:21 of vostell begin: SUN IN YOUR HEAD—
décollaged program (tv picture)

6:22 cinemascope (camera: edo jansen) pictures
dissolving themselves

6:23 pictures in many layers, exploding pictures—
décollage sounds accompany the film

6:24 (taped sounds of the moment of objects'
destruction): light bulbs,

6:25 vacuum cleaner, the opening of a seltzer bottle

6:26 pouring out of water, motor of a toy

6:27 leafing in a book, etc—during the showing of
the film: within

6:28 the audience, cleaning teeth, gargling—seven
transistors with an erased

6:29 program—light shocks, shots, laughter, light
explosions, actions

6:30 reflexes (mr anybody climbs over the seats)
applause ends . . . .

6:31 . . . j: wonderful! owner of movie house con-
fused—v flashes bulbs, b shows his postcards

6:32 public starts to sing *Das Wandern ist des
Müllers Lust*

6:33 v shoots his flashgun

6:34 someone complains: we could do without this part of the trip

6:35 trip through small gardens with arbors—past the most beautiful

6:36 bread bakery (architect: jaehrling) b shows his postcards, v flashes

6:37 this trip is an indeterminate, open composition, evolving out of

6:38 pluralistic possibilities

6:39 of thought and material—all different

6:40 growing out of the impossibility of ever wanting to co-ordinate

6:41 anything or everything—absence of focal point—décollage is an invasion

6:42 of a situation—décollage is more disruption than destruction!

6:43 vohwinkel shunting station title: "130 à l'heure"

6:44 railroad right-of-way between small gardens with arbors

6:45 tennis courts, crowds, inquisitive housewives, football·players

6:46 children, rr police, collision, two locomotives with an automobile (mercedes 170)

6:47 at the same moment r in a gas mask offers the people shashlik

6:48 many voices: is that all, because of this all the fuss?

6:49 reporter b to a housewife: can you tell me anything

6:50 about what you have just seen, are you affected in any way

6:51 by what you have seen?—housewife (laughing): for god's sake!

6:52 reporter: yes, that was a trial for an automobile

6:53 a quick test for heart and stomach!—housewife: HAHAHAHAHA!

6:54 (drawn-out laughter)—little boy: daddy, you say it!

6:55 (everyone silent)—housewife: the quick test was done before

6:56 you came, we waited for an hour for it, that was the test—departure

6:57 m gives out cards with actions and requests written on them to

6:58 the people on the bus—a few carry out the instructions

6:59 for instance: CALL OUT LOUDLY: MAR-VEL OF MANAGEMENT

7:00 CALL OUT LOUDLY: IVORY FLAKES

7:01 GAZE AT EVERYTHING BLUE IN YOUR NEIGHBORHOOD

7:02 THINK ABOUT CHINA

7:03 COUNT THE MONEY IN YOUR POCK-ETS IMMEDIATELY

7:03 DO YOU PREFER FUNDAMENTAL LAW TO WELFARE LAW?

7:04 during the trip through the city i have the following thoughts:

7:05 the audience is probably of the widespread opinion that

7:06 décollage is the philosophy of destruction—those who think that

7:07 way in this bus forget the daily traffic accidents, airplane

7:08 crashes, natural phenomena which, against men's wishes, present

7:09 destruction—to increase these happenings would be unreasonable

7:10 i am much more interested in enlightenment

7:11 through décollage, which reveals the absurdities

7:12 and unfair demands of life by taking daily occurrences out of

7:13 context—the public thus reacts through shock and by reflection

7:14 leipacher garden shop, cronenberger street—beverly hills-like

7:15 situations—title: MORNING GLORY!

7:16 today's picture newspaper (10 cents)

7:17 is ground up

7:18 in three waring blenders

7:19 with eau de cologne, black pepper, and flower seed

7:20 (kind: morning glory #7)—after this the blended newspaper

7:21 will be poured on the flower beds between the audience—this

7:22 happening repeats itself until the entire newspaper is décollaged

7:23 b eats a piece of headline (in oil and with salt): COMMUNICATIONS!

7:24 IS CHAOS HERE ALREADY?—audience creates jungles of opinion!

7:25 HAHA—or applause . . . comments on the headlines before

7:26 they disappear in the mixer

7:27 headlines from the tabloid of july 14, 1963:

7:28 BUCHER: THAT WAS ILLEGAL

7:29 AUTOMOBILE BRIDE NO 2 MARRIES
7:30 22 US SENATORS AGAINST AID FOR SOUTH VIETNAM
7:31 THE SOLDIER 1963: QUIET WITH BEARD
7:32 NEW US TELEPHONE THINKS
7:33 SPECTATOR OF LIFE
7:34 A PORTION OF DEFENSE FUNDS FOR SPORT
7:35 NEW BMW A BOMB
7:36 I SCREAM FOR GOD
7:37 IVORY FLAKES SECRET FORMULA X IS THE REAL THING FOR LAUNDRY CARE
7:38 BREAD IS HOARDED IN MOSCOW
7:39 one blender stops working
7:40 whistles
7:41 again thoughts:
7:42 décollage is your digestion
7:43 décollage is your accident
7:44 décollage is your death
7:45 décollage is your analysing
7:46 décollage is your life
7:47 décollage is your change
7:48 décollage is your weight reduction
7:49 décollage is your problem
7:50 décollage is your tv trouble
7:51 décollage is your feces
7:52 décollage is your fever
7:53 décollage is your sweat
7:54 décollage is your confusion
7:55 auto lineup for the next situation
7:56 décollage is your trials and tribulations
7:57 décollage is your failure
7:58 décollage is your abortion
7:59 décollage is your nerve
8:00 décollage is your rupture
8:01 auto convoy driving through fields and woods
8:02 valley
8:03 hahnerberg quarry
8:04 winding roads, mud—dark
8:05 décollage is your disappointments
8:06 décollage is your being put out of the way
8:07 décollage is your unmasking
8:08 décollage is your spot cleaner
8:09 décollage is your dismissal
8:10 décollage is your pain
8:11 décollage is your hasty passage
8:12 décollage is your unveiling
8:13 décollage is your being décollaged

8:14 décollage is your uneasiness
8:15 a stands on the stone wall—at 8:15 the transmission of
8:16 "the smallest show on earth" begins
8:17 a spectacular with international cast
8:18 theme of the performance: looking into the distance—dialogue
8:19 concerning seeing into the distance to be heard in the entire
8:20 valley—j and v scramble up on the stone wall to décollage
8:21 the tv picture—audience speechless—people stand about 240 feet from the faint image
8:22 ....
8:23 ....
8:24 ....
8:25 ....
8:26 ....
8:27 explosion of picture screen—title: IS THAT THE WALL?
8:28 everything dark—with the help of an auto searchlight, the
8:29 audience finds its way back
8:30 to the
8:31 cars
8:32 in order
8:33 to begin
8:34 the trip
8:35 to wuppertal
8:36 city
8:37 .....
8:38 large workhorse garage
8:39 fully occupied buses drive into dark garage
8:40 people cannot leave the buses
8:41 v and b décollage objects in the dark
8:42 on the bus windows
8:43 ..... the people inside take these things to be acoustical
8:44 shocks—more of same
8:45 stream of water
8:46 cleans the buses in the
8:47 darkness
8:48 the ladies are uneasy
8:49 the driver in saxonian dialect: maybe this isn't over?
8:50 passers-by are wound up in transparent plastic
8:51 someone in the audience wants to climb up on the elevated train
8:52 THINK IT YOURSELF—wants to tie up the train

251

8:53 gives up halfway

8:54 spectator loses a piece of jewelry on the plaza lawn

8:55 all search

8:56 departure

8:57 factory basement once used as an air raid shelter

8:58 title: ART AND THE PRETTY HOME— or

8:59 TELEVISION MUST BE LEARNED

9:00 twelve happenings and situations run off at the same moment

9:01 in four different rooms, in which the audience stands around

9:02 or takes part in the action—wall of living people are shot at

9:03 in green, red, and blue—first aid in germany (first aid kit

9:04 from woolworths)—r, legs in sand and typewriter under water,

9:05 writes something—s and k twist: YA YA—k twists on toy tanks

9:06 js plays tapes of previously recorded reactions

9:07 ab projects nude photos on men's white sportcoats and attaché cases

9:08 j lies in bed and eats candy, meditates about art galleries

9:09 b ties the vacuum cleaner around his body and cleans the

9:10 atmosphere—ej takes pictures

9:11 m writes numbers on various body parts of the audience

9:12 v transforms the tv set into a sculpture with barbed wire

9:13 t puts the estate of an uncle in order

9:14 dialogue which mr b is forced to listen to in a cold-cuts booth

9:15 where the two bus drivers and the policeman sat:

9:16 1st to 2nd: what's the meaning of all this?— they're all mad

9:17 2nd to 1st: i don't understand it either!

9:18 policeman: if my kids did this sort of thing, i'd beat their

9:19 behinds sore

9:20 . . . . .

9:21 in the meantime the performance continues in the cellar

9:22 factory manager to v: . . . that's the end . . . or do you want to go

9:23 into the other cellar?

9:24 v: no, but into the neighboring cellar!

9:25 audience permits

9:26 itself

9:27 to be led

9:28 into another cellar

9:29 and permits itself (surprisingly)

9:30 to be (flashing lights)

9:31 locked in

9:32 behind fences

9:33 silence—murmuring—suddenly, lp: vostell, that's enough

9:34 for me . . . i want out . . . let me out . . .

9:35 i'm nauseated!

9:36 v: you have a strong imagination, your reaction pleases

9:37 me—other woman: twenty years ago it was like this in koenigs-

9:38 berg—zs runs up and down the wire fences with a police

9:39 dog—title: IS BIRMINGHAM IN THE UNITED STATES?

9:40 people go to the buses

9:41 departure

9:42 for

9:43 galerie parnass

9:44 garden behind gallery

9:45 on the lawn

9:46 standing separately

9:47 electric cookers, several of them,

9:48 on which there are frying pans,

9:49 cake tins,

9:50 cooking pots, all filled with plastic toys that

9:51 are melting

9:52 from the heat

9:53 this happening stinks

9:54 title:

9:55 DECOLLAGE A LA VERTICALE

9:56 little by little the objects in the gallery

9:57 are served at the banquet

9:58 which

9:59 are donated in honor of this day by

10:00 the university of avant-garde hinduism

(translated by Mildred Feingold)

Plan for *You*, 1964

YOU: A DECOLLAGE HAPPENING FOR BOB AND RHETT BROWN

Performed at a swimming pool, orchard, and tennis court at King's Point, N.Y., April 19, 1964.

The Basic Idea:
The public is brought face to face, in a satire, with the unreasonable demands of life in the form of chaos, and is confronted by the most absurd and repugnant scenes of horror to awaken consciousness. It is not important what I, Vostell, think; what the public itself takes away, as a result of my images and the Happening, is important.

Situation and Site:
A path, so narrow that only one person can pass at a time, winds toward a swimming pool. The ground underneath is covered with colored advertisements from Life Magazine. The path goes through a woods, along a tennis court, through a dark, stinking stable. Here is a hidden loudspeaker that greets each passer-by with "YOU, YOU, YOU!"

Farther on there is a glistening white swimming pool. In the deep end sparkles a pool of water in which stand several typewriters. All around the edge of the pool lie huge, clear plastic sacks filled with brilliant yellow, red, green, and blue dye. There is a box of plastic toy water pistols nearby, full of the same bright-colored dye. Three color TV

sets, each placed upon a white hospital bed, are showing three different baseball games, each with a different distortional pattern. The sound, however, is normal. In a large refrigerator a Beatles record is playing.

Lying on a trampoline, Lette Eisenhauer is enveloped in a transparent, flesh-toned garment upon which are painted the female parts. Two huge beef lungs beside her bounce. On the other side of the pool, a naked girl lies on a table, a vacuum cleaner tank on her body, motor running, embracing and fondling the machine.

Leaving the pool area, the people walk along a blue path at the edge of an orchard, and encounter obstacles of trees, shrubs, vines, etc. You see a large, empty field with bare fruit trees standing in black earth, on which flicker five hundred mourning candles. Now you reach the tennis court, painted a bright yellow. At one end of the court stands a bicycle on which there is a playing black-and-white TV set. In the center of the court is a circular enclosure measuring seventy feet in diameter and covered over by a white parachute. Hidden on the yellow court are forty orange-colored smoke bombs. Lying about on the ground are four hundred pounds of beef bones.

The Unfolding of the Events:
All the people crawl or walk along the path. In the swimming pool, a mountain of people is growing and becomes multicolored from the dye pouring from the burst plastic sacks, human beings, gallons of blue, red, and yellow color, bones, all in a jumble. Some of the people tie bones on their bodies. Lette Eisenhauer bounces on the trampoline beside the beef lungs and becomes blood-smeared.

Down in the dyed water, Tomas Schmidt writes on the typewriter "YOU, YOU, YOU, YOU ..."

The Beatles record plays in the closed refrigerator. The TV sets are on. Twenty to thirty people snake their way on their stomachs to the tennis court. In the field flicker the white mourning candles.

All the crawling people lie about on the yellow tennis court. All the walking people stand within the circular enclosure and sprinkle yellow paint on the supine bodies. The TV sitting on the bicycle bursts into flame. The people put on gas masks and watch a three-minute program on the burning set. The TV explodes.

The white parachute floats down upon the people as the whole area fills with orange smoke from the bombs. Everyone within the enclosure receives an envelope. The people are now free to find their way out of the enclosure. They go through the woods back to the buses which will return them to New York City.

Instructions to the People:

Please find your way to the swimming pool, either crawling or walking.

At the pool, take a pistol filled with color.

Please crawl into the swimming pool.

Lie down on the bottom of the pool and build a mass grave. While lying there, decide whether or not you will shoot the other people with the color.

Allow yourself to be tied to the beds where the TVs are playing.

Free yourself.

Crawl or walk down the blue path to the yellow tennis court. Say hello to Bob Brown and ask him for a little bag of yellow color. Sprinkle the color on the blue people who are lying on the yellow tennis court.

Open the envelope and read the card inside while the parachute is falling.

Put on a gas mask when the TV burns and try to be as friendly as possible to everyone.

(translated by Dorothy Schulz)

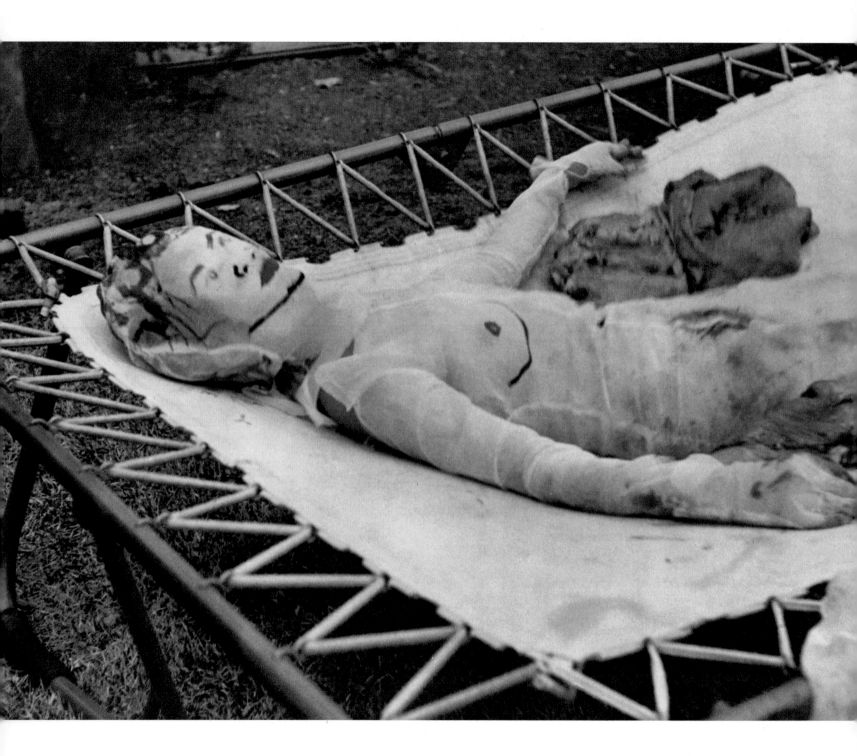

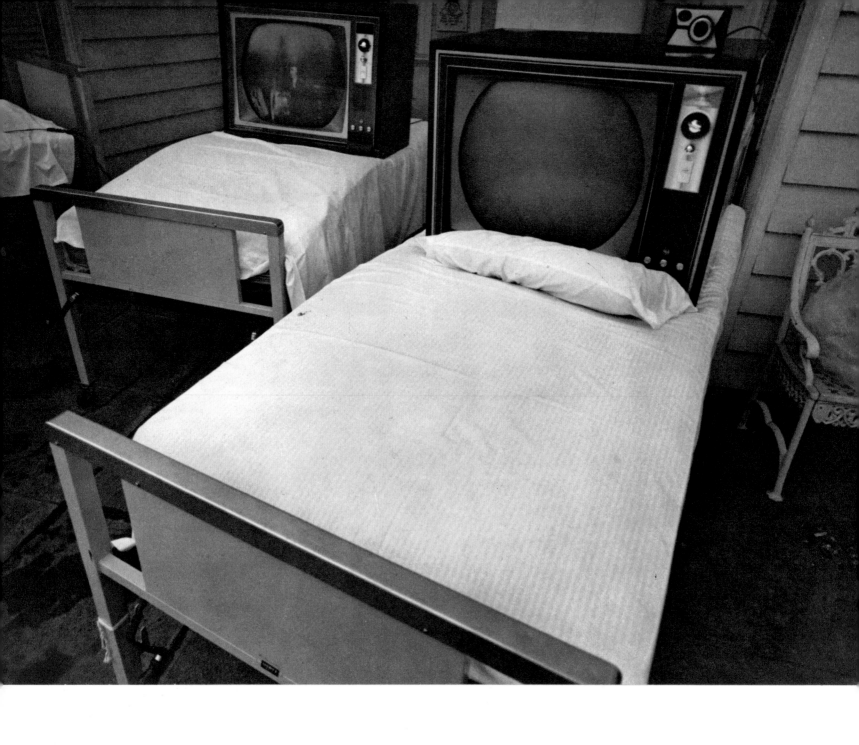

INSTRUCTION CARDS (44 per set):

1. Head lights (high beam, low beam) on (1-5), off.
2. Parking lights on (1-11), off.
3. Foot-brake lights on (1-3), off.
4. (Right, left) directional signals on (1-7), off.
5. Inside light on (1-5), off.
6. Glove-compartment light on. Open (or close) glove compartment (quickly, with moderate speed, slowly).
7. Spot-lamp on (1-11), move (vertically, horizontally, randomly), (quickly, with moderate speed, slowly), off.
8. Special lights on (1-9), off.
9. Sound horn (1-11).
10. Sound siren (1-15).
11. Sound bell(s) (1-7).
12. Accelerate motor (1-3).
13. Wind-shield wipers on (1-5), off.
14. Radio on, maximum volume, (1-7), off. Change tuning.
15. Strike hand on dashboard.
16. Strike a window with knuckles.
17. Fold a seat or seat-back (quickly, with moderate speed, slowly). Replace.
18. Open (or close) a window (quickly, with moderate speed, slowly).
19. Open (or close) a door (quickly, with moderate speed, slowly).
20. Open (or close) engine-hood, opening and closing vehicle door, if necessary.
21. Trunk light on. Open (or close) trunk lid (if a car), rear-panel (if a truck or station-wagon), or equivalent. Trunk light off.
22. Operate special equipment (1-15), off.
23-44. Pause (1-13).

MOTOR
VEHICLE
SUNDOWN
(EVENT)

(TO JOHN CAGE)
SPRING/SUMMER 1960
G. BRECHT

Any number of motor vehicles are arranged outdoors.

There are at least as many sets of instruction cards as vehicles.

All instruction card sets are shuffled collectively, and 22 cards are distributed to the single performer per vehicle.

At sundown (relatively dark, open area incident light 2 foot-candles or less) the performers leave a central location, simultaneously counting out (at an agreed-upon rate) a pre-arranged duration 1 1/2 times the maximum required for any performer to reach, and seat himself in, his vehicle. At the end of this count each performer starts the engine of his vehicle and subsequently acts according to the directions on his instruction cards, read consecutively as dealt. (An equivalent pause is to be substituted for an instruction referring to non-available equipment.) Having acted on all instructions, each performer turns off the engine of his vehicle and remains seated until all vehicles have ceased running.

A single value from each parenthetical series of values is to be chosen, by chance, for each card. Parenthetic numerals indicate duration in counts (at an agreed-upon rate). Special lights (8) means truck-body, safety, signal, warning lights, signs, displays, etc. Special equipment (22) means carousels, ladders, fire-hoses with truck-contained pumps and water supply, etc.

Some of the following works have been printed by the artist privately and others by FLUXUS Publications for limited distribution.

TIME-TABLE EVENT

to occur in a railway station

A time-table is obtained.

A tabled time indication is interpreted
in minutes and seconds (7:16 equalling,
for example, 7 minutes and 16 seconds).
This determines the duration of the event.

Spring, 1961
G. Brecht

THREE AQUEOUS EVENTS

- ice
- water
- steam

Summer, 1961

273

TWO EXERCISES

Consider an object. Call what is not the object "other."

EXERCISE: Add to the object, from the "other," another
object, to form a new object and a new "other."
Repeat until there is no more "other."

EXERCISE: Take a part from the object and add it to the
"other," to form a new object and a new "other."
Repeat until there is no more object.

Fall, 1961

THREE TELEPHONE EVENTS

- When the telephone rings, it is
  allowed to continue ringing, until it stops.

- When the telephone rings, the receiver
  is lifted, then replaced.

- When the telephone rings, it is answered.

Performance note: Each event
comprises all occurrences
within its duration.

Spring, 1961

TWO DURATIONS

● red

● green

THREE WINDOW EVENTS

opening a closed window

closing an open window

FIVE PLACES

Write the word EXHIBIT on each
of five small cards.

Set each card in a place fairly
distant from the others.

EXERCISE

Determine the center of an object or event.

Determine the center more accurately.

Repeat, until further accuracy is impossible.

SMOKE

●   (where it seems to come from)

●   (where it seems to go)

277

all night

at three

on the floor

in the water

CLOUD SCISSORS

music, dance, stories, games, puzzles, jokes, defections, solutions, problems, biography, questions, poems, answers, gifts

to Robert Filliou   from George Brecht

from the tree

the yellow ball

The above was printed on the outside of an envelope; the phrases of two or three words were contained within on separate cards, and meant to be arranged in any order.

at home

EWEY

Three types of Happening projects are included here.

The first, *In Memory of Big Ed,* was straight reportage of a situation.

The second, *Museum Piece,* was an environmental study,

in which a museum, its exhibits, and the space around it were treated as a

vast musical instrument. *Summer Scene* was a conversion,

in which the audience, after participating in a children's game,

reexperienced it as a ritual, and then as an abstraction.

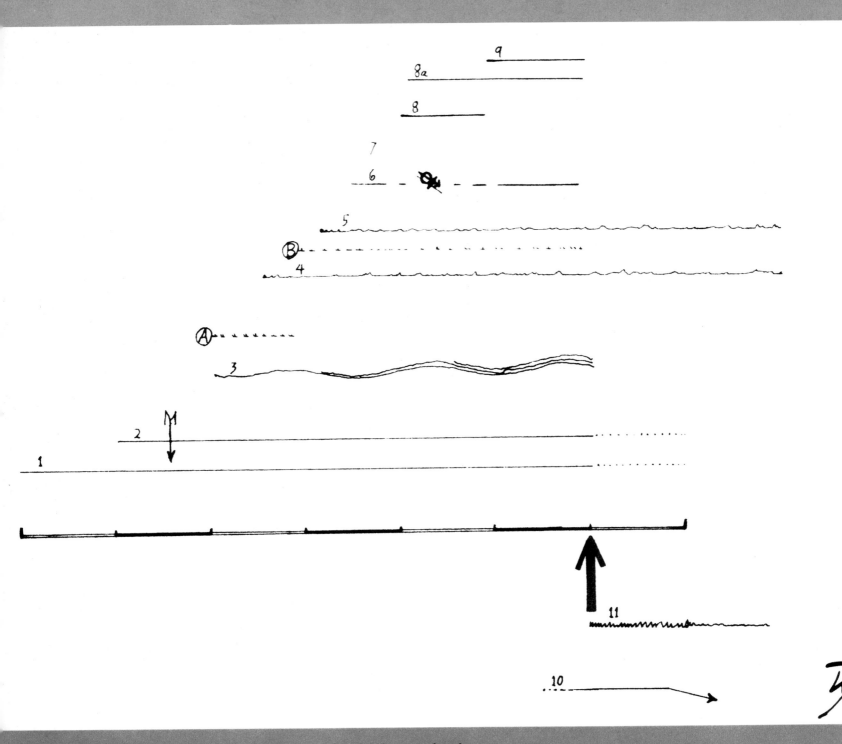

Rule at bottom of score indicates minutes. Certain aspects of timing were altered
in performance. Composition and preparation time: four days.

IN MEMORY OF BIG ED

This piece was performed in Edinburgh on "Theatre of the Future" day of the International Drama Conference, September 1964, at request of Conference organizers, as one of two demonstrations of Happenings the other by Allan Kaprow Marowitz prepared his resolution. Overall planning was by Lewsen, Boyle, and myself.

1) Charles Marowitz submits "straight" resolution to the conference, asking that precise symbolism of *Waiting for Godot* be established.

2) Charles Lewsen questions him from floor.

M) Microphone brought to Lewsen.

A) Tape: Cable puller's sounds come on speaker outside hall.

3) Organ on very low notes.

4) Large face put into light at top of hall.

5) Sheep skeleton hung on screen with design of Festival.

B) Tape: Sound collage of conference onto loudspeakers in hall.

6) Three figures begin staring in windows high in dome. At signal they call down "Me! Look at Me!"

7) On speaker's stand Carol Baker, who has been staring at Allan Kaprow seated in back of hall, gets up, takes off her coat, and starts back across tops of seats. When she reaches Allan, they leave the hall.

8) Nude model Anna Kesselaar is wheeled across loft on light stand.

8a) Electrician crosses ledge at top of hall.

9) Bagpiper crosses top balcony.

11) At large arrow there is a cut off of sound and movement. The reflecting curtain for TV behind the speaker's stand is dropped and Mark Boyle's Assemblage of phrenology head studies appears.

meanwhile:

10) A pregnant woman with two children, who entered the hall some moments earlier, mounts the speaker's stand. They examine "the various exhibits" and leave.

Medverkande
från Studentteatern:

Per Andersson
Stig Billberg
Sören Brunes
Stefan Böhm
Tomas Böhm
Birgitta Eklöf
Göran Gunér
Ingegerd Hellner
Rose-Marie Larsson
Björn Melander
Rolf Olle Nilsson
Börje Remberger

från Balettakademien:

Suzanne Fahlén
Mikaela Geggen
Lena Lindegård
Maria Sinclair
Kajsa Viberg

Inger Tverin
Karin Thulin

Christer Boustedt   altsax
Jan Carlsson   slagverk
Bengt Ernryd   trumpet
Kurt Lindgren   kontrabas
Lars Werner   piano

Form och ljus: Sören Brunes
                         Rolf Olle Nilsson
Ljustekniker: Christian Nowak
Projektioner: Pi Lind o. Staffan Olzon
Talare: Lars Egler
Kompositörer: Jan Bark
                         Henrik Otto Donner
                         Folke Rabe

Regi: Ken Dewey

Moderna Museet i Stockholm
Den 7 april 1964

Producerad av FYLKINGEN

TRIBUTES &
FLOOR PLANS

Excuse me but | your
              | my

things are in | my
              | your   room.

TRIBUTES - FLOOR PLANS

Excuse me but are in your my/your things /my room.

S
T
O
C
K
H
O
L
M

7
A
P
R
I
L

1964

kl 19.30

church →

E - Mobile
F - Garden
G - Offices
H - Magazine (Dressing Rm. area)
I - Cafeteria

C III - For tape recorders + perf. standby area.

DE
DII

Tributes

Interval

E.m.b. y/m

t.a.i.

m/y r.

1 - Arrival: Audience parked drive-in fashion facing mobile ((alder). Those on foot shown to cars with empty seats.

2 - Piece: MOBILE/Brass instr. CHURCH TOWER MUSIC (E).

3 - Entrance: Audience into museum, tickets taken (D-I). One small automobile joins queue, is admitted.

4 - Distrib: Audience to seats in FLOOR PLAN sec. (A,B,C).

5 - Pieces: Performers move thru, play to + with environ, light shows, tapes. With small perf's. various of us make unannounced + unidentified private TRIBUTES to people who've influenced our work.

6 - Move: Audience to (C), form chair rows. Blupper music.

7 - Interval: GARDEN/ROOF music piece.

8 - Piece: E.m.b., etc. (C).

9 - Move: Audience to (A) floor sit, stand, lie.

10 - Piece: STAIRWAY/WINDOW (D).

11 - Exit.

Overall scheme for *Museum Piece*. Arabic numbers correspond to time segments. Arrows indicate transitions. Capital letters indicate the different areas in use.

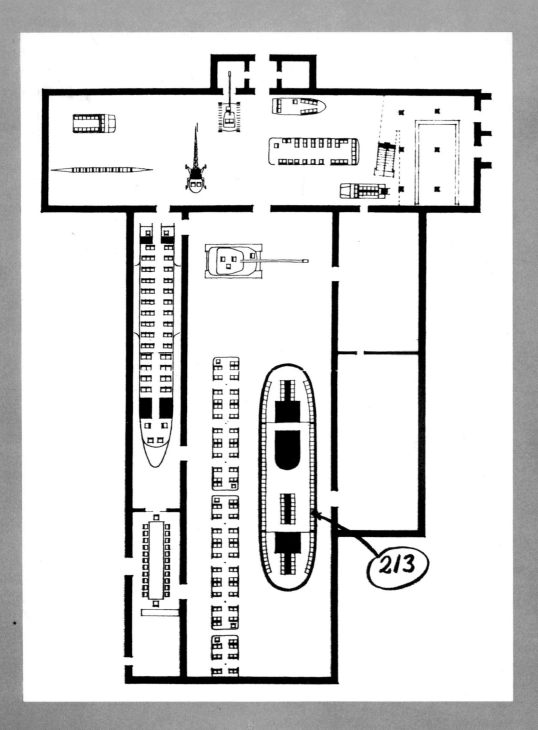

Floor plan of museum printed on program. A number with an arrow directed each program holder to a specific seat. All seats were arranged according to how one would sit in some moving object, such as a ferryboat, tank, caravelle, etc. These were placed in relation to artworks from a visiting American Pop Art exhibition, e.g., the bus waited for George Segal's *Bicycle Rider* to move, helicopter was under the guns of Roy Lichtenstein's war picture, *"O.K. Hot Shot, O.K.!"* The audience entered during segment 4 of the overall scheme and remained seated throughout segment 5.

A dialogue took place between Birgitta Eklöf (standing) and trumpet player Bengt Ernryd (not shown). It was not jazz and poetry. She simply said things to him and occasionally he played small sounds back to her. Lots of silence, watching, waiting.

Lars Werner in "Excuse me but—" section, hunting for collaborators.

Rose-Marie Larsson was on the lead end of a 180-foot history-of-the-world-in-rags train. Her marriage to the small automobile followed.

SUMMER SCENE

Performed July 5, 1964, at Jyväskylä, Finland, at a summer arts festival. The following is the outline on which the game conversion was based.

STAGE I: Posters, announcements, press conferences, rumors
    Stress: Happening for participants only
        A children's game, "Capture the Flag," will be played
        Then variations on the game will be done in the same way variations are done on melodic line in jazz

STAGE II: Audience arrival, tickets, program
    Include: 1) Map of playing area showing boundaries
         2) Reminder all are participants

STAGE III: Audience collected inside auditorium
    1) Go over rules. Stress all talking to be in whispers
    2) Introduce leaders
    3) Divide into teams
    4) Tell them to go to cemetery when tagged (dead)
    5) Give starting instructions

STAGE IV: Audience in position for game; leaders give battle plan

STAGE V: The game
    1) Dead are collected into cemetery
    2) End signal: early reports and interviews

STAGE VI: Ritual retelling
    1) Victory procession
    2) Burying with flowers

STAGE VII: Battle of the bands

STAGE VIII: Making of personal flags

NOTE: During stages III through VII, unrelated musical and visual events counterpointed the action. At the instruction session they were outright interruptions, later they became progressively more subtle.

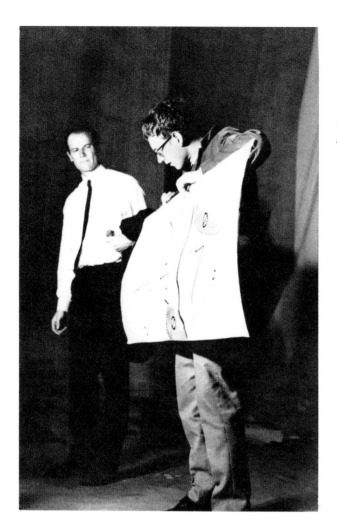

Mikko Pyhälä shows map of grounds and translates descriptions and rules.

Participant makes a personal flag. These were put on buildings and fences in the area.

At cemetery, the dead were given paper bags for their heads. In a last-minute change the victory procession was made by the dead, and the leader of the dead instead of the winner was buried in flowers.

MILAN KNÍŽÁK, *Short Carting Exhibition*, 1963. The Czech writer, Jiri Mucha, tells me that once every couple of months, Prague homeowners make a neat pile of whatever they want to throw away—old furniture, clothes, crockery, etc.— outside their doorways, for removal by the Sanitation Department. Knížák's work took place on such a day, with the artist and his friends taking up the collection earlier than the removal trucks. Going around with wheelbarrows and carts, they naturally found marvelous things, and these in turn were dumped into a large new pile in the street and also left for garbage removal. Mr. Mucha believes that this adventure alludes to a medieval custom in which an especially disliked person was ridiculed by the local youths, who would load his rooftop in the middle of the night with enormous quantities of junk.

AN INDIVIDUAL DEMONSTRATION

Performed in Prague in 1964.

Stand still in a crowd. Unfold a piece of paper, stand on it, take off your ordinary clothes and put on something unusual, e.g., a jacket half red, half green, with a tiny saw hanging from the lapel, a lace handkerchief pinned to the back.

Display a poster on which is written: "I beg the passer-by, if possible, while passing this place to crow."

Lie down on the piece of paper, read a book, tear out the finished pages. Then stand up, crumple the paper, burn it, sweep up the ashes carefully, change your clothes, and leave.

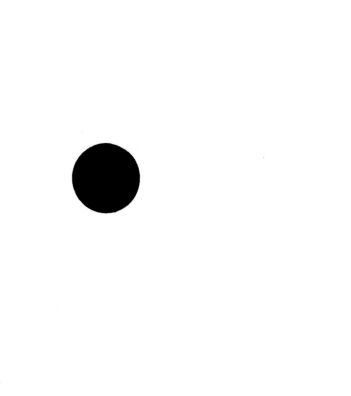

DEMONSTRATION FOR ALL THE SENSES

Performed in Prague in 1964. Soňa Svecová, Vít Mach, and Jan Trtílek, all members of the Art of the Actual group, collaborated.

The organizers of the demonstration wear unusual clothes instead of jewels—articles of daily use or pieces of fancy material sewn on ordinary clothing, parts of clothing painted with some color, preferably red or white, and the like.

Every newcomer is given a thing to carry in his hand at all times, e.g., a piece of cutlery, a plate, glass, vase, teapot, piece of clothing, shoe, or the like.

Walking down the street they pass a room with an open window, near which a man sits at a laid table and eats.

They go on, and are led into a small room, where they are locked in and left in inactivity for anything from five minutes up, according to their reaction or indifference. A great deal of perfume has been spilled on the floor of the room.

They are now let out. What has happened to them was only preparation, a disturbance of their normal state of mind.

The walk goes on. They encounter things—parts of furniture, clothes, etc. A musician lies on the ground and plays a violin.

They reach a small place and are put in the middle of a circle. Around them the organizers of the demonstration run, shouting, roaring, cutting across, driving round on motorcycles and in cars.

A chair comes down from above. They look at it and point. Then a man comes and puts the chair on a pedestal.

All fall to the ground. After a minute another man comes, takes the chair down, and sits on it.

All get up.

The participants are appealed to, to arrange a number of objects in a row. Each participant stands behind his own object.

They are then asked to pick up their objects and rebuild the row 20 centimeters farther on. This is repeated as long as desired, according to the reaction of the participants.

Now they walk back. A man stands at a wall, glazing a window. As soon as he is finished, he breaks it. In the middle of the street a woman lies on a mattress, listening to a transistor radio. The participants stop and are presented with a book, from which each one tears a page. Then they return their objects and leave.

The first, active part of the demonstration is now finished. The second ends in a fortnight, and is different for each participant. Everything that happens to him during this period is a second demonstration.

TWO UNPERFORMED DEMONSTRATIONS

Demonstration One

In a room, where the radio and the water tap are on, the window and the door open, sit down on a chair in the middle and sit motionless for at least five minutes.

Now turn off the radio and the tap, shut the window and the door, and leave.

Thus you are ready to stand still in the middle of a crowd.

Demonstration Two

This Demonstration is the contribution of Soňa Svecová.

I am on a tram.
The tram is crowded with people.

I am smartly dressed, nicely coiffed and made up, so that I create the impression of being a lady.

After ten minutes, I suddenly ask the people standing near me to please make room. I place a little white rag, about 50 centimeters square, on the ground and stand on it, after removing my shoes. From my luxurious beaded handbag I take shoe polish, a brush, and a rag.

I polish my shoes nicely and then put the equipment back into my handbag without saying a word, and proceed calmly to my destination. Or, if anyone asks me what I am doing, I politely offer the shoe-polishing materials.

KAPROW

PUSH AND PULL: A FURNITURE COMEDY FOR HANS HOFMANN

Prepared for the Museum of Modern Art's traveling exhibit "Hans Hofmann and His Students," April 1963. First printed in Décollage *(ed. Vostell), No. 4 (1964), Cologne.*

Instructions:

Anyone can find or make one or more rooms of any shape, size, proportion, and color—then furnish them perhaps, maybe paint some things or everything.

Everyone else can come in and, if the room(s) are furnished, they also can arrange them, accommodating themselves as they see fit.

Each day things will change.

Points of View:

Think of subletting someone's apartment. How can you get rid of the fellow when he is in every piece of furniture, every arrangement? Do you like living with him? Imagine it unfurnished. What would you do—buy some things (if so, what style?), scrounge some off the streets, ask your relatives or friends (which will remind you of them?) . . . Perhaps live without furniture instead. As for the question of style, why not have everything totally unrelated to everything else—shape, color, period, arrangement, etc.?

Can it be done? Do you like candy canes? Then why not paint everything in stripes? Or, better, like twelve different types of candy canes? Maybe dots, billions of them, baby dots, mommy dots, daddy dots, pink, brown, snotgreen, white, orange, shocking-red, Dā-glo blue—all over everything, floors, ceilings, inside of drawers, in the sink, on the silverware, on the sheets and pillowcases. . . . Do you prefer round rooms, tall ones, hexagonal ones, caves, lean-to's, rooms without windows, skylights? Suppose you liked eating off the floor (some people are that clean, I'm told)—it could be carpeted with food at all times. Design it like a Persian rug and you could eat your way through the designs, right across the room, making new ones behind you as you went along. Maybe, after all, formality is the thing. Then carefully choose a big chair, a little one, a bigger table and a very small lamp, and push them and pull them around until they make a significant composition. The significance is determined by having both a calculated and an intuited reciprocity obtain between every push in one direction, and every pull acting against it in another direction. Significance may be achieved within either a structure of symmetries, in which each push–pull relation is made of near-equals; or a structure of asymmetries, where the push–pull relation is realized from near-equivalences. But one caution! Don't sit on the chairs, because this will destroy the composition. Unless, of course, you once again start pushing and pulling everything around until it works right. Repeat when you leave. Consider whether or not you're a red-head and dressed in Kelly green. Are you fat, fatter than the table? In that case, quickly change your clothes if the small chair's color doesn't correspond; and also lose some weight. What about the kids? And their toys? I'd suggest allowing for a variable proportion of three yellow toy ducks to be considered equivalent to one medium-sized violet dress (softened by black hair, brown eyes, and leopard-skin bag). Now these relationships will be seen to exactly balance the combined density of the orange large chair, the brownish mantle ornament, and the beige stripe running around the baseboard. You mustn't neglect the spaces in between the furniture and how they figure in the total space. They are, in fact, "solids" of another order, and each negative area is colored and qualified by the punctuating components (tables, chairs, etc.) around it. The interactivity between negatives and positives, furthermore, may be so equalized as to produce a higher neutrality than the biases of the separate elements. Properly handled, a silence of perfect ineloquence will result. On the other hand, the positives or negatives may be accented, producing a ruler–ruled relation. This in turn may be enhanced or neutralized by closed-field or open-field concepts: closing a door or opening it, for instance, will contain or break the boundary of the structure. Now, since these generalizations are made concrete by the frequent occurrence of children's toys being left in any ordinary room, it is only necessary to stay out of the room when the toys are there and vice versa. However, don't suppose the conclusion here is "each to his own." The further question is "who knows how to compose forms?" If "form" is now too much for you, why not chuck it all and take the pure leap? What is a "pure leap"? (The word "comedy" in the title of this Environment isn't necessarily humorous—though it may be—I had in mind Balzac's "Human Comedy.") Instead of "forms" try simply an idea like: rooms full of people contrasted with empty rooms; one, maybe a hockshop, the other, a monk's cell. . . . A sunset-colored room against a blue-Monday one. . . . Or, the "room" made by your own feelings wherever you decide to sit down in the woods. Aren't these "forms" also? Is a nude woman on a bed a better form than a pink coverlet on a bed? Which is more personal? If the forms of the furniture express "you," what are you going to do about others? When visitors come and you draw up chairs for them, don't you express "them" a little? What happens to the room? Who is right? Should rooms be lived in or stared at? I have heard of some people who have antique chairs you mustn't sit on because they'll collapse. Don't move that ashtray because it expresses Daddy so well just where it is! But maybe the smell of mushroom soup cooking will heighten the color-chords on the walls, particularly the candy-cane stripes. I find that Rhythm-and-Blues on the radio goes fine with soundless newscasts on TV. Try it out if you really want to compose your rooms! Did you ever think of arranging rooms for darkness, that is, for night-time, when you go to bed and see only dim shadows? A room for feelies only! Wet surfaces, rough, sandpapery objects, other things as soft as foam rubber to run your toe into getting to the bathroom at 4 A.M., silks slithering across your cheek, very large solids like cedar chests for braille identification. This should be a thoughtful problem, and it would develop all the senses except the eyes. How long does it take to develop artistic senses? Why not ask an interior decorator?

If they wish, exhibitors may hereafter add their own "points of view" on the blank cardboards included in this crate, using black enamel and brush, as indicated. This way the crate will change by additions as the Environment will change by interpretation and alteration.

To the Exhibitors: [sent separately]
Following are the title, instructions, and some general thoughts concerning my contribution to this show of former students of Hans Hofmann. Each exhibitor has the right to set up the Environment-Happening or disregard it. Either he may do it himself or appoint some person to do it for him. All the information printed here is also contained in a wooden crate, on large sheets of cartonboard.

This crate should be exhibited at all times with the top open and visitors to the exhibition should be invited to leaf through its contents. Next to the crate there should be a very low platform or coffee table where the cartonboards can be put as they are read. Request visitors to replace them in order after reading them. Perhaps a placard could state this, and somewhere nearby could be displayed photos of the piece as it was arranged in New York City, and also those taken of each new version of it. After a time, the record of the conception's morphology from exhibition to exhibition should prove instructive. From time to time an attendant might check the crate to see if the visitors have kept the cartonboards in order. If an exhibitor decides to have the Environment-Happening made for his particular show, the crate should be placed near the entrance to the room(s). Under no circumstances should this typewritten copy be shown to the public, since this would defeat the purpose of the crate. The latter is conceived as a kind of file cabinet that is made to be transported easily. At the same time, it invites the visitor to involve himself physically with the idea of the situation, at least in its preliminaries. Implied here, and of course in the actual Environment-Happening, is the wish to by-pass the habit of "sshh, don't touch," useful with respect to older art but an impediment to understanding certain traditions that have recently begun to develop. I am most interested in the handshake between the artist and others. The museum or gallery director can now be instrumental in bringing this about.

[From reports, I gather that this arrangement has not worked out optimally. In an exhibition atmosphere people are not geared to enter into the process of art. Hence, this kind of work is much better off away from the habits and rituals of conventional culture. A.K.]

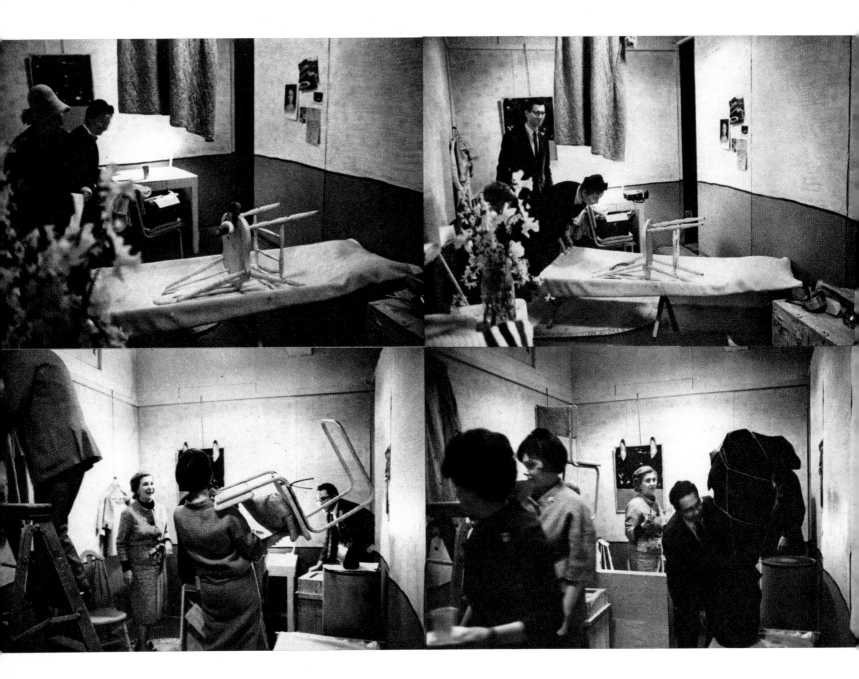

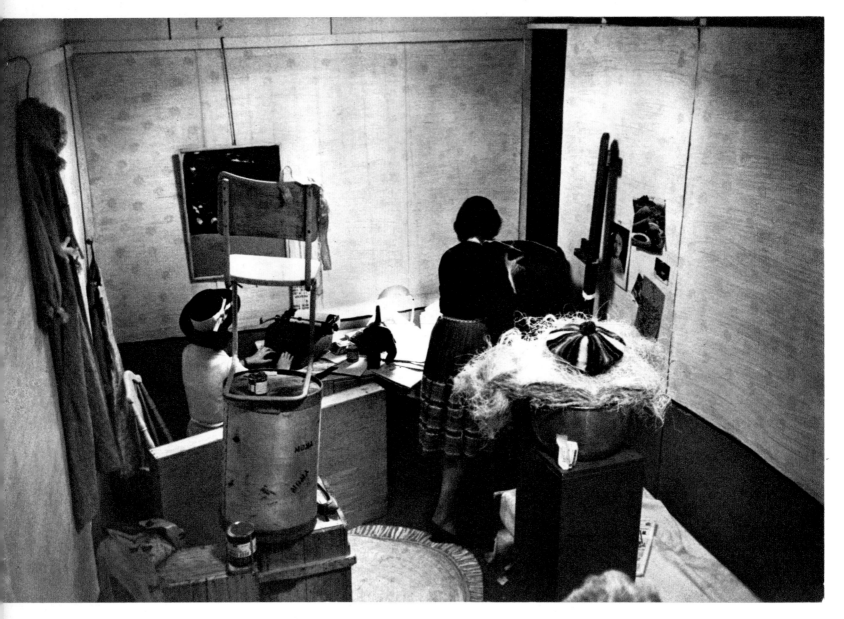

These photos show two rooms I constructed in a warehouse, interpreting in one way the generalized instructions of this work. The first room was brightly lit, a bedroom, consisting mostly of yellow objects, relieved by a red band around the upper walls. The second room, like an attic, was lined with tar paper, and was illuminated by a small overhead light well and a soundless television set on the floor behind a wooden crate. Boxes, old clothes, and other junk littered the space.

The public arrived and began moving everything; an exchange took place between the objects of both rooms. Soon there was a mess. Some older women resented this and began to straighten things up, as though they were cleaning house. Other women joined in. Gradually, the two rooms returned to a state approximating what they originally were, and the cycle was complete. I played no part in this action.

The dark attic room.

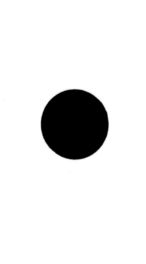

HOUSEHOLD

A Happening commissioned by Cornell University. Performed May 1964. There were no spectators at this event. Those taking part in it attended a preliminary meeting where the Happening was discussed and parts distributed.

Setting:

A lonesome dump out in the country. Trash heaps all around, some smoking. Parts of dump enclosed by old, red tin fence. Trees around rest of it.

Sequence of Events

I. 11 A.M. Men build wooden tower on a trash mound. Poles topped with tarpaper clusters are stuck around it.

Women build nest of saplings and strings on another mound. Around the nest, on a clothesline, they hang old shirts.

II. 2 P.M. Cars arrive, towing smoking wreck, park outside dump, people get out.

Men and women work on tower and nest.

III. People circle dump, out of sight among trees and behind tin wall, wait.

Women go inside nest and screech.

Men go for smoking wreck, roll it into dump, cover it with strawberry jam.

IV. People's voices call "Hey! Hey! Hey!" all around dump.

Men go to women, put on shirts, squat down and watch them.

People very slowly start coming in toward car, still calling "Hey! Hey!"

Women screech.

V. Women go to car and lick jam.

Men destroy nest with shouts and cursing.

People, coming in, start to pound pots and blow police whistles in slow unison.

VI. Men return to women at wreck, yank them away, eat jam with fingers, slap white bread all over sticky stuff, eat with their mouths.

Women scream at men, "Bastards! Bastards!"

People advance, banging and whistling.

VII.   Women destroy men's poles and tower, laughing, yelling "Watch this! Watch this!"

Men eat bread.

People advance, banging and whistling.

VIII.   Women go to heaps of smoking trash, call sweet-songy come-ons to men.

Men fan out, creep low to ambush women.

People advance, banging and whistling.

IX.   Women jump men, rip off shirts and fling them into smoking trash, run to men's tower mound.

Men roll on ground laughing loud: "Hee! Hee! Hee! Haw! Haw!"

People advance, banging and whistling.

X.   Women take off blouses, wave them overhead like hankies, each singing own Rock 'n' Roll tune and twisting dreamylike.

Men hurl red smoke flares into smoking trash heap.

People circle smoking jam-car, become snent, squat down, eat jam sandwiches.

XI.   Men go to wreck, take sledge hammers from people, pick up battering log, begin to demolish car.

Women watch from a distance and cheer men for every smash.

People eat silently and watch.

XII.   Men jack up car, remove wheels, set fire to it, sit down to watch, light up cigarettes.

People light up cigarettes, watch car burning.

Women run out of junkyard, waving blouses, gaily calling "Bye! 'Bye! G'bye! 'Bye!" They get into cars, drive away with horns blaring steadily till out of earshot.

XIII.   Everyone smokes silently and watches car until it's burned up.

Then they leave quietly.

SOAP

1ST MORNING

CLOTHES DIRTIED BY URINATION

1ST EVENING

CLOTHES WASHED

(IN THE SEA)

(IN THE LAUNDROMAT)

2ND MORNING

CARS DIRTIED WITH JAM

CARS CLEANED

ON A BUSY STREET

(IN A CAR-WASH)

(IN A PARKING LOT)

2ND EVENING

BODIES DIRTIED WITH JAM

BODIES BURIED IN MOUNDS

AT THE SEA EDGE

BODIES CLEANED BY THE TIDE

NOTES TO SOAP

1st morning and 1st evening: Each person privately soils some article of his own clothing. This is essential, for it refers to one's real experiences as an infant. In this act the person mingles his own water with the water of the sea or laundromat and consequently makes the cleansing of his clothing inescapably personal.

2nd morning: Cars should be methodically and thoroughly smeared with jam, within sight of passers-by. The washing should be done as diligently. If a commercial car-wash is used, one should have this done as though nothing were out of the ordinary. Any questions asked should be answered in as noncommittal a way as possible.

2nd evening: A vacant stretch of beach is best. Either couples or individuals may perform this. There should be long distances between each individual or couple. In the case of couples, one person covers the partner (who is preferably naked) with jam, digs a hole for him (or her), covers him (or her) with sand to the neck, and sits quietly watching until the tide washes the partner clean. They then depart.

Commissioned by Florida State University. Performed in Sarasota on February 3 and 4, 1965. Like the preceding work, this was first discussed in conference and then performed only once, without rehearsal and without spectators. Appropriate sites were chosen by the participants shortly before performance. Actions indicated in parentheses are alternatives given to participants: either or both could be enacted.

RAINING

BLACK HIGHWAY PAINTED BLACK
RAIN WASHES AWAY

SHEETS OF WRITING SPREAD OVER A FIELD
RAIN WASHES AWAY

PAPER MEN MADE IN BARE ORCHARD BRANCHES
RAIN WASHES AWAY

LITTLE GRAY BOATS PAINTED ALONG A GUTTER
RAIN WASHES AWAY

NAKED BODIES PAINTED GRAY
RAIN WASHES AWAY

BARE TREES PAINTED RED
RAIN WASHES AWAY

NOTES TO RAINING

Black highway painted black: A lonely stretch of highway should be selected, and a time when it is only sporadically traveled, such as 3 A.M. Black watercolor in large buckets is splashed and brushed onto as long a piece of road as possible. When it next rains, the painters may choose to return to sit at the edge of the black strip.

Paper men made in a bare orchard: Constructions or papier-mâché images should be made in the bare branches just before they bloom in early spring. When it next rains, the slow collapse of these paper men into dripping sogginess may be watched by the builders.

Sheets of writing spread over a field: An elderly woman might sit by herself and watch her old love letters wash away; a painter might spread out his worst drawings and laugh in the drizzle. These papers should be personal, in any case.

Little gray boats painted along a gutter: Children (or adults) should paint images of boats in a gutter; when it rains, they may watch them dissolve and disappear down the sewers.

Naked bodies painted gray: When it rains, adults or children may paint themselves or each other's naked bodies on a city rooftop, at the beach, or at a country place.

Bare trees painted red: Here again, an April orchard is best, just before the leaves emerge. A gasoline-powered spray gun, using red watercolor, is most efficient for covering large areas of branches, but if preferred, brushes may be used. When it rains, the dripping color will probably stain the ground around the trees.

Scheduled for performance in the spring, for any number of persons and the weather. Times and places need not be coordinated, and are left up to the participants. The action of the rain may be watched if desired. (For Olga and Billy Klüver, January 1965.)

PHOTOGRAPHIC CREDITS

Numbers refer to pages.

Ay-O, *42, 43*

Max E. Baker, *8, 24, 83*

Carlo Bavagnoli, LIFE Magazine, © Time Inc., *88, 89*

Paul Berg/St. Louis Post-Dispatch, *317–21*

Rudolph Burckhardt, *5*

Cameraphoto, *229–32*

Francesco Cantarella, *41*

Don Cook, *11*

David Gahr, *109, 110*

W. F. Gainfort, *53*

Michael G. Gilligan, *12*

Sol Goldberg/Ithaca Journal, *324–37*

The Solomon R. Guggenheim Museum, *41*

Ken Heyman/Meridian Photographics, *139, 143*

Martha Holmes, © Time Inc., *3, 34, 90*

George Franklin Hurych, *7, 13, 23, 50*

Scott Hyde, *44, **45**, 49*

A. Kouzel, *6*

Terry S. Lindquist, *92*

Robert R. McElroy, *7, **14**, **15**, **18**, 25, 37, 52, 54, 55, 57, 59, 60, 62, 63, 65, 76–**80**, **93**, **97**–100, 118, 119, 122, 124, 127, 131–33, 138, **140**, **141**, 144*

François Massal, *236, 238–**40***

Peter I. Moore, *22, 26–28, **38**, **69**–71, 85–87, 111–13, 116, 117, 123*

Hans Namuth, *10, 142*

Obchodni banka a.s. Prikopy, Prague, *300, 302, 303, 309*

Claes Oldenburg, *19, 31, **32**, **91***

Mikko Phyälä, *295, 296*

Eric Pollitzer, *36, 130*

Portable Gallery Press, Inc., ***114**, **137***

Pressens Bild, *289–292*

Edwin M. Sabol, *75, 104–**6***

THE SCOTSMAN, Edinburgh, ***284***

Shunk-Kender, *94, 126*

Lawrence Shustak, *134–36*

Pablo Volta, *235, 237*

Robert Watts, *67*

Courtesy Jiro Yoshihara, *212–224*